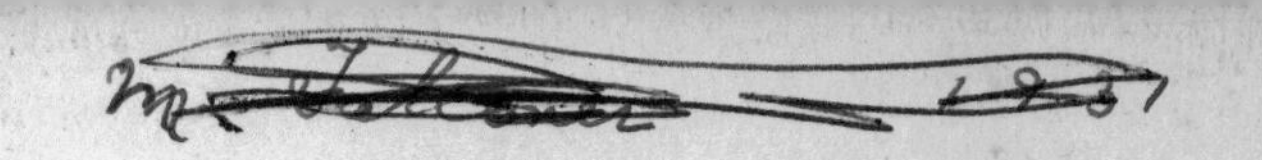

KU-367-903

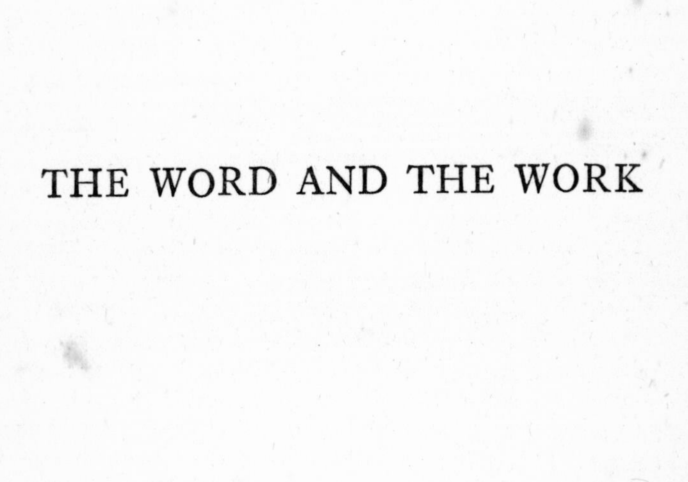

THE WORD AND THE WORK

THE WORD AND THE WORK

BY

G. A. STUDDERT KENNEDY, M.A., M.C.

Rector of S. Edmund King and Martyr, Lombard Street.
Chaplain to H.M. The King.

WITH AN INTRODUCTION BY
THE LORD BISHOP OF LONDON

SIXTH IMPRESSION

LONGMANS, GREEN AND CO LTD.
39 PATERNOSTER ROW, LONDON, E.C.4
NEW YORK, TORONTO
BOMBAY, CALCUTTA AND MADRAS
1926

Made in Great Britain

INTRODUCTION

THIS book will make people *think*. It will give them, to use the author's phrase, " A pain in the mind." Too many of us do not think at all; others do not think deeply enough. It is hard to say which is the most irritating: the shallow optimist or the shallow pessimist. In Christian circles the shallow optimist is the most common. He does not really face the tragedies in life, the inequalities in human lots, the injustice by which the innocent so often suffer for the guilty.

No one who has been through what the author has been through during the War and since can help facing it, and the usefulness of this book consists in this: that it shows it to be a possibility, even when you have faced everything, to keep your faith, tremblingly, but still to *keep* it in a good God.

" In the beginning was the Word "—everything is contained in that sentence, according to the author, who paraphrases it thus: " Right at the heart of the ultimate reality there was in the beginning, is now, and ever shall be, world without end, a Person expressing a rational purpose which man can, in some measure, understand." The whole book is a thesis upon this, and, although the opening chapters will be found difficult to some, all will understand and appreciate the most moving chapters with which the book closes.

The words of one of our most beautiful Mission hymns:

"In the Cross, in the Cross, be my glory ever,"

have rung in my own ears from the Missions which I often conducted in earlier days, and these chapters sound the refrain again.

It *is* only in the Cross that we find *any* answer to the sin and suffering of the world, and then only if we proceed from gazing at the Cross to taking it up ourselves. The book is studded with pieces of poetry. Sometimes they are quotations, and sometimes, I think, the author's own creations. These beautiful lines sum up the teaching of the sixth chapter:

"Peace does not mean the end of all our striving,
Joy does not mean the drying of our tears;
Peace is the power that comes to souls arriving
Up to the light where God Himself appears.

* * * *

Give me for light the sunshine of Thy sorrow;
Give me for shelter the shadow of Thy Cross;
Give me to share the glory of to-morrow:
And gone from my heart is the bitterness of loss."

[p. 73]

If the book begins by producing pain in the mind, I hope sincerely that it will end by bringing some sort of peace to the many to-day terribly tried and troubled by the problems which life and death present.

A. F. LONDON:

FULHAM PALACE,
S.W.

TO THE UNEMPLOYED MEN AND WOMEN
OF GREAT BRITAIN
THIS BOOK IS DEDICATED
WITH SYMPATHY AND RESPECT

We begin, then, with a conception of reality as existing in many grades, each of which finds its own completion or perfect development only in so far as it is possessed or indwelt by that which is above it. But we then notice that each depends for its actuality upon those which are below it. Matter itself, as experienced by us, can be reduced to what is simpler than itself, whether, α, β, or γ particles or still more simply to space-time. Life is unknown except from living organisms which are matter informed by life. Mind is unknown except in reasonable living organisms. Spirit is unknown except in conscientious, reasonable, living organisms. . . . The universe will be approached less as a problem (or theorem) in geometry, more as a drama or symphony, and as a society in process of formation.—WILLIAM TEMPLE ("Christus Veritas").

CHAPTER I

In the beginning was the Word.—S. JOHN i. 1.

THERE are no words that have ever been penned by the hand of mortal man which contain profounder wisdom than the opening verses of the Fourth Gospel. If I ask you this Lent to concentrate your thought upon the passage, it is not with any idea that we can together reach the hidden depths of its meaning, or exhaust its inexhaustible treasures of Truth, but because no honest thought about it, after prayer for the light and guidance of the Holy Spirit, can fail to be fruitful of real results.

The opening phrase "in the beginning," carries our minds not merely back to the beginning of time, but beyond time and space altogether. It lifts us above things to the ultimate meaning and value of things. It would be better to translate it: "Right at the heart of the ultimate reality," or "At the back of everything." The word "was" is also timeless, implying a mode of existence without beginning and without end, and we could best render it by the phrase: "Was in the beginning, is now, and ever shall be world without end," by which we strive to express eternity. The WORD, whether we take it as Greek or Hebrew in origin, cannot mean less than a Person expressing a rational purpose which I can, in some measure, understand. It is certainly Personal, and the idea of a Person who is "a word" must mean a person who expresses a rational idea or purpose in such a way that it can be understood by men. Thus if we translate the five Greek words as "*Right at the heart of the ultimate reality there was in the beginning, is now, and ever shall be world without end, a Person expressing a rational purpose which men can in some measure understand,*" we get nearer to the meaning of the words, even though it sound cumbrous and queer.

The old seer warns us that if we are to understand aright the sublime story which follows, the story of the Incarnate Christ, we must be prepared to go down to the very roots of reality. We must take up our stand before the great "other than ourselves," of which we are conscious, the world of men and things, and must ask ourselves "What does it mean?" and "Why does it exist?" He lays down at once the foundation-stone of the Christian faith about the universe, which is also the foundation of any rational faith that can be held about it whatsoever, Christian or non-Christian. He does not begin with Christ, but moves by force of rational necessity from Life to the need of a meaning for Life, and from that to the meaning of Life as revealed to him in the blaze of light that shone in the face of Jesus Christ. *The world and the life of men in the world have a meaning and a purpose.* This is the great assumption, the initial act of faith, which is at once the highest result of thought, and the foundation of all thinking. Without it life, in any sense beyond animal existence, and thought about life, are impossible. At its heart the world is not mad, but sane. The stars above our heads, and the stones beneath our feet, are for ever talking, and talking sense, sound sense, and not cruel nonsense. That is the bare minimum of faith for man. If that goes everything goes, and we can neither live nor think about life, we can only take a long time to die. It might seem as though this assumption were so obviously true as to be platitudinous and unimportant. But anyone who thinks that must be either very young or exceptionally fortunate. Most men and women over thirty have been through times when it was by no means obvious.

I do not know whether any of you who read these words have ever been through what I think is one of the most searching and terrible experiences this troubled life affords. Have you ever had a friend with whom converse was sheer joy because of his intelligence, sympathy, and understanding; a friend with whom speech was scarcely a necessity because eye met eye, and smile answered smile, finishing the unfinished sentence, answering the unuttered thought, revealing that most glorious of all things—an active and reasonable mind? Then have you known the day when your friend "Went out of his mind," as we say? It is a tragic and torturing phrase: "He has gone off his head," "He is out of his mind." No one who has not known it at first-hand can appreciate the creeping horror those words convey. Converse is transformed from pure joy to pure agony. One comes away, aye runs away, with pity and repulsion tearing at one's heart, and the whole fabric of one's faith in life tottering on its base. There is nothing in life which is at once so piteous and repulsive as insanity. Well, what the great Teacher says is that we need not, must not, feel that horror in our converse and communion with the world in which we live. There is reason in it. It is not mad.

But there are now, and I fear there always have been, a large number of people who found and find even that bare minimum of faith difficult if not impossible to accept. I shall never forget an old lady in France who, because she could not imagine what life would be like outside the village where she had always lived, or conceive of dwelling in any other cottage but that which was her home, clung to both even when the fighting-line was drawn within a mile. She had a little plot of land outside the village, and two cows which she used to lead by a cord. We soldiers, if I can be called a soldier, had a kindly feeling towards her, and used to call her "Madame." Often when the evening came we used to see her leading her two cows up the village street, and would hail her as she passed. I think she valued those jolly deep-throated shouts of "Bon soir, Madame." Men were still men, and there was kindness on the earth. Then one day when the village, which up to then had escaped bombardment, was heavily shelled, we came upon her sitting on the roadside near to her two cows which had been literally torn to pieces, wiping her wounded face, and crying through her tears: "Le bon

Dieu, il est mort ! Le bon Dieu, il est mort ! " (" The good God's dead.") There is no sense, no meaning in the world ; it is mad, it is a dirty, cruel, muddled mess, that grinds and crushes living things to death. That was how it seemed to her.

There we come to it. Right from the Gospel of S. John to the soul of a peasant woman in her hour of bitterness. So we always come from the deepest Truth to the simplest life. Truth which is so lofty that it cannot come down to earth is not truth at all, but the product mostly of intellectual conceit that loves obscure and twisted subtleties. It is from this last and awful darkness that the Gospel light is sent to save us. We must cling to that first and final act of Faith : " In the beginning was the Word." With it we are safe ; without it we are damned to the outer darkness of despair. If life has never driven us to the very edge of that darkness, if we have never known what it means to clutch at our faith as a climber clutches at a jutting rock or tree-root on the edge of a ravine, with a desperate prayer that it may hold, we are among the lucky ones in this strange life, and should go softly and with grateful hearts, made pitiful because they are at peace. Moreover, we should remember constantly that our first duty, the only *raison d'être* of our existence, is that " through the tender mercy of our God whereby the day spring from on high hath visited us, we may give light to them that sit in darkness, and in the shadow of death, and guide their feet into the way of Peace."

If all that our religion does for us is to save us from the great abyss, if we are deaf to the cry of those who are reeling over the edge, clinging wildly to some last hope, or lying in the depths ; if it does not fill us with the longing to save others, it is a fraud, it will not last. Life will get us yet. " Let him that thinketh he standeth take heed lest he fall." If you feel no longing to right wrongs, to war against injustice and cruelty, to defy tyrannies, to abolish ugliness and dirt, look out ! You are standing on a rotten piece of ground ; it will give way beneath you when the hour comes, and you will go down. No rites, no ceremonies, no soft music and stately ritual will avail to save you. They will go down with you, and you will stand by a broken altar with filth upon the fair linen cloth and cry in vain for your comfortable Christ. I tell you I have been there, and I know. You cannot stop at crying: "What shall I do to be saved?" You must go out into the world, crying: "What can I do to save?"

All ound you there are men and women who are well-nigh esperate. You must learn to hear them cry. They do not all speak plainly of their need. They do not know what they want. Some curse and swear, some laugh, some sneer, some dance defiance of despair; all but the weakest wear some pitiful disguise to hide their secret sorrow from the mockery of men. If you take men and women as you find them, and have no eyes to see them as they are, you walk in the world through a land of dreams, and never reach reality at all. Whatever else this odd world is, it is neither conventional nor commonplace. As usual, extremes meet, the cynic who sneers and the theoretical idealist who smugly smiles, carry on their warfare in a phantom universe that centres round themselves. One gleam of God's reality would lay them both stark dead.

Three months ago when I landed from America and reached Paddington Station one dreary Sunday night, I was accosted by a young man, who touched his hat to me, and asked if he could carry my bag. The touching of his hat made me sick to start with. You see he did not do it because he really respected me, or thought me worthy of it. He was crawling for a job. That is disgusting. I felt ashamed all over. My very bones blushed. There are men I love to take off my hat to; it is a joy to do them reverence. If ever the day comes when no man removes his hat to another, and is the better for doing it, it will be a bad day for mankind. We shall never all be equal except by levelling down. Mankind can never be levelled up without ceasing to grow, for growth depends, and always has depended, largely upon the exceptional individual, the personality to whom the rank and file of men look up, and whom they delight to honour. We do not lose our dignity by honouring the truly honourable. But that was not the reason of this hat-touching business; it was crawling, cringing for money. It was servility. I do not and did not blame him. Necessity knows no law. But I was ashamed, and am ashamed. If any man touches his hat to me, not because he respects me, but because necessity puts him in my power, he degrades himself and me. Both slaves and slave-drivers are an abomination to the Lord. If you really like that sort of things your soul is in danger. I let him carry my bag, not that I really wanted it—I could have carried it myself—but because I wanted to talk with him. We went down the street, and talked of many things. At last I asked him whether he believed in God, or went to a place of worship. There came into his face a look which was in itself the most dreadful reply to such a question—a grin that was half a sneer, and he poured out at me his philosophy of life. It was just bitter, naked, disillusioned cynicism. The War and the Peace had finished all that for him. Every man for himself and the devil take the hindmost was the truth about life. There was no room in the world for Gentle Jesus, and that sort of stuff. Here was another for whom the first foundation act of faith was difficult if not impossible. He did not believe that the ultimate reality was reasonable, or that there was any meaning in life. Peace—or what we called Peace—has as many victims as War, it damns as many souls to the outer darkness of despair. It is the task of the Christian Church to save them.

We are often told that the Church has nothing to do with social questions ; that there is no social Gospel ; and that we should stick to our real business of saving individual souls. There is truth in the warning, but in the way it is often put it is just the half-truth which is the most dangerous sort of lie. It is perfectly true that we must not mistake the Kingdom of Comfort for the Kingdom of Christ, and suppose that if we could secure adequate wages and decent conditions of life for everyone our work would be done, but the souls we have to save are incarnate not disembodied souls, and there are conditions of life which are soul-destroying, not merely because they are painful, but because they are essentially degrading, inhuman, and wrong. All poverty is not degrading. There is a poverty which, as Christian saints have often shown, can set men free, and endow them with real wealth, the wealth of joy in simple things. But there is a degrading and destructive poverty which starves and stunts the human soul and makes for death, not fulness of life. Against that the Church, if she be true to herself, and true to her Lord, must wage ceaseless and unremitting war.

The poverty of men such as this one whom I met, and there are millions of them, is prostitution of the human personality. It is a branch of the white slave traffic, and it is our duty to stamp it out of the world, not merely by rescuing individuals who are compelled to prostitute themselves by crawling for employment as this man was compelled to do for the sake of his wife and children, whom the dole could not keep, but by devoting ourselves to the reform of those conditions which force him into this position. There are miles and miles of our modern cities and villages, too, which in the eyes of Christ are as beastly as a brothel, and for the same reason, they are the symbol and the sign of wholesale traffic in human souls. The miners' cottages in many of our colliery villages tell us, just as plainly as though it were printed in great flaming letters on a hoarding, that here are "Souls for Sale," and you need not bid too high, either; there are plenty of them. Living and working under such conditions it is well-nigh impossible for many of them to cling to their first act of Faith, and believe that at the heart of things there is a Person expressing a reasonable purpose that they can in some measure understand. They see no evidence of it, and it is difficult to show them any, either.

For my part, when I am tempted to doubt the goodness of God, and the essential sanity of the universe, the first challenge that I have to meet is the challenge of Beauty—the sheer beauty of God's world. The longer I live the more it means to me. It is a perpetual rebuke to the rank ingratitude of unbelief. When my soul gives up the fight for faith and tries to sneer at life, God hoists again the flags of dawn, or blows his trumpet from the hills, and brings me humbly back again.

Up to these purple hills, O God,
I lift my longing eyes,
Thy gaunt and silent sentinels
Against the sunset skies.

Their great heads bowed upon their breasts
Their helmets tipped with flame,
They stand to guard the mystery
Of Thy most Holy name.

All gnarled but empty are their hands,
They wield nor sword nor spear,
And yet in trembling reverence
My stubborn soul draws near.

Bright blades of beauty are their swords,
The majesty of years,
The challenge of eternity
To tide of time and tears.

The paltry prizes of my sin
Show shameful, poor, and mean,
O mercifully merciless,
Unclean! I am, Unclean!

Christ, Thou white Christ upon the hills,
I dare not come to Thee,
I can but beat upon my breast
And clutch at Calvary.

It is possible indeed to become sentimental and unreal about beauty, possible to compose manifestly artificial rhapsodies about the glory of God in the beautiful things of the world, but to deny the healing, pleading, and power of beauty is to sin against the Holy Ghost, and to give the lie to one of the most poignant and positive experiences of life.

So it seems to me. Nor do I believe that I am alone in this. Only a very small minority of the human race can be called intellectual. There are millions of men and women who could not follow an argument beyond its simplest stages to save their lives, but almost all men are more or less artistic. Again and again I found in France, among the mass of ordinary men whom the bitterness of life was driving every day to the very edge of the abyss of despair, that what called them back again to their vague but valid faith in the final goodness of God was the glory of a sunset or a dawn; the colour of some wayside flower; or the laughter in the eyes of a peasant child in the village where they went to rest. They needs must love the highest when they saw it, and could not withhold their tribute of "Well Done" to God's accomplishment, and that is the root of worship in the soul of man. I believe from the bottom of my heart that to the great mass of mankind if they are to be healthy and sane, that is, if they are to be saved, *beauty is as necessary as bread.* "If you have two loaves, sell one and buy a lily," says an old Chinese proverb. A piece of wisdom that has its roots in the nature of God and of man. Seventy-five per cent. of our people are out of touch with organized religion, and with the worship of God, and one of the chief reasons for this is that our industrial civilization blasphemes against the beauty of God. We have come to regard Beauty as a luxury for the few, and not as an absolute necessity for the many, and have cut off millions of our people from their chiefest natural means of grace. The cumulative effect of this excommunication of the masses is disastrous. The results of bad housing, overcrowding, and of the barbarous ugliness of our cities are not only ruinous physically and morally, but spiritually. They corrupt the souls of men, and undermine their faith in the goodness of God.

Beauty does not lie only in the eyes of the beholder, nor only in the thing beheld; it lies in a subtle sympathy and harmony between the two. There is beauty in the world because "right at the heart of the ultimate reality there was in the beginning, is now, and ever shall be a Person expressing a rational purpose which mortal man can in some measure understand." But the world in which multitudes of our people live, the world of dirty, dingy streets, gaunt, ungainly factories, and ramshackle hovels run up anyhow, reveals no rational purpose of any kind. It is a symbol, not of divine order, but of human, all too human, chaos, a chaos of disordered and unregulated passions, lust of power, and lust of gold, pugnacity, vanity, and pride. It is not merely outwardly ugly, but inwardly vile.

It is essentially evil. We comfort ourselves by saying: "They are used to it"; and that is true, the most terrible truth of all. They do get used to it, reconciled to it, reconciled to evil and ugliness, and ready to believe that it is the real world. That is the final horror. The most dreadful thing about the people of the underworld is their content. But, thank God, it is not very deep; there is rebellion in a hundred millions souls all over the world to-day. East and West, wherever the great machine goes out, there are signs of passionate protest against this murder of the human soul. The protest is dangerous; it is as terrible as a volcano, it may tear the whole fabric of civilisation into ribbons, destroying the good with the bad, the true with the false, unless it is guided right. It may become a rebellion against God and His Christ, unless Christians can make it a rebellion in the name of God against the evil and ugliness that blaspheme the beauty of His Love.

If you take this book with you into Church, and kneel down in the silence before the altar of God, listen to the voice of the world. I always hear it; it is like the voice of the sea, a moaning voice of many waters crying out for God.

Peace we were pledged, yet blood is ever flowing,
  Where on the earth has ever Peace been found?
Men do but reap the harvest of their sowing,
  Sadly the songs of human reapers sound.

Sad as the wind that sweeps across the ocean,
  Telling to earth the sorrow of the sea;
"Vain is my strife—just empty, idle motion,
  All that has been is all there is to be."

So on the earth the time waves beat and thunder,
  Bearing wrecked hopes upon their heavy breasts;
Bits of dead dreams and true hearts torn asunder,
  Flecked with red foam upon their crimson crests.

Can you hear that voice and still believe in God? Still believe that in the beginning was the WORD? Then you have got the Truth, go out and tell it, go and live it, go out and suffer for it; that is the will of Christ. But if your altar is a refuge, if you put your fingers in your ears, to shut that awful voice outside; if you have built a private sanctuary for the comfort of your little soul, then look out! It is going to fall on you; the winds of God are coming to blow it all away, and you may cry after it with many tears, but it will not come again. It is a nasty mean little place, and the wrath of God's Love will burn and burn and burn it until there are not even left the ashes of regret.

CHAPTER II

And the Word was with God, and the Word was God. The same was in the beginning with God.—S. JOHN i. 1 and 2.

AN old Indian teacher used to say: "The dumbness in the eyes of animals is more touching than the speech of man, but the dumbness in the speech of man is more agonizing than the eyes of animals." Human speech when it aspires to express anything beyond the lowest levels of thought and feeling is an effort to express the inexpressible. Even the speech of our Lord is that; hence that pathetic cry: "He that hath ears to hear let him hear." It is at once a warning to man, and a prayer to God. The weakness of words was one of the woes that went to make up Calvary, as it has gone to make the cross of every real poet, prophet, preacher, and teacher ever since the world began. The shadow of that Cross lies dark upon the glory of S. John.

"This person expressing a rational purpose was eternally with God, and, indeed, was God, and yet it is truer to say that He was with God." He is face to face with the final mystery, and, as usual, words fail him; he cannot say it. He wants to say with all the power of his being that *God can and must be known,* that men can hear and have heard Him speak, that our knowledge of God is a reality, the greatest and most necessary of realities, here and now upon this earth. He wants to protest, and protest with passion, against the unknown and unknowable God so dear to the natural man, the "Supreme Being," whom everybody acknowledges but nobody cares a rap about. Formal and consciously formulated atheism is scarcely ever real atheism. It is generally the worship of some neglected aspect of God in mistake for the whole of Him. Professing atheists are often religious people, protesting against some caricature of God which they suppose, or have been taught, is His reality. Real atheism, which is either sin or nervous disease, may be ready to acknowledge that there must be a God, but denies that He is or can be known by man. A passionate blasphemer is often as near to the Kingdom of God as Saul the persecutor was to Paul the prophet, when he witnessed the stoning of Stephen. He blasphemes because he half believes. Real atheism denies that the Word is God, denies that there is any rational purpose in life which men can enter into and understand.

This denial, if it be persisted in, means the death of the human soul. It lies at the root of all sin. For the man who denies that life has a purpose of its own there is nothing left but to invent a purpose for life. This is what he inevitably does. He takes the world and tries to make it serve his purpose and submit to his will. Since he cannot know God, he worships the only God he can know, which is himself, and the inevitable result of this idolatry is disillusion and despair, and the greater the man is the more awful is the tragedy. The supreme example, perhaps, is Napoleon, whose uniquely powerful natural genius enabled him to blast, pound, tear, and torture the world in order to shape it to his will, only to find that it would not bend, but that he must break, and listen at last to the judgment of the sea as it cried against the cliffs of S. Helena. The world is full of Napoleons, only different because they are so puny and so small, scheming, planning, twisting and torturing the world in a million futile blundering ways to make it serve their little human ends, until their natural force abates, and life throws them aside to grumble and to die. That is the monotonous miserable story of a million million lives, and its constant repetition is the most searching challenge to faith in God of which I know. A challenge and yet a confirmation, for it does proclaim and reproclaim the necessity of God, a God who can be known and loved, with whom we can, in however small a way, co-operate, becoming in S. Paul's audacious phrase, "fellow-workers with Him," and so finding life.

The growth of modern knowledge has, in many subtle ways, strengthened the temptation to that real atheism which denies that God can be known, or the purpose of life in any real sense be understood by man.

Science has revealed to us the vast infinities of space and time, and added so much to the immensities of the universe that our minds reel back amazed and afraid. We cry out, with a new fear that perhaps there is no one to hear our cry, "What is man that Thou should'st be mindful of him or the Son of Man that Thou should'st visit him at all." Moreover, not only has our conception of the universe become greater, but life in it has become more complex. Not merely is the individual daunted, cowed, and baffled by the gigantic spectacle of nature, as science reveals it to him, but he is swallowed up in the multitude of our teeming populations, and bewildered by the intricate network of human relationships in which he must become entangled if he is to live at all. The temptation to give it all up as a bad job is tremendous. It comes in all sorts of guises. It borrows the raiment of humility, and appears as a prophet denouncing human pride. What can we ridiculous creatures who crawl about on the surface of a minor planet set for a time in the timeless and spaceless eternity of things, know about the meaning and purpose of creation? It is only our presumption, and fatuous conceit that deceives us into supposing that we know, or can ever know, the meaning of it all. Do not common honesty, reasonable reverence, and proper humility demand from us a frank acknowledgment that it is utterly above and beyond us, that we neither know nor can know anything as to its ultimate meaning and purpose.

This attitude, moreover, appeals to the natural sloth which is in us all. Sir Almroth Wright has said that "a pain in the mind is the prelude to all discovery," and it is certain that we never think or strive to solve a problem unless it hurts us to leave it unsolved, and many of us will not move unless the unsolved problem hurts us very badly. We need a pain and a very sharp pain, either in the mind or somewhere else, before we are willing to face the effort of thought. If we can by any means soothe the pain, and, as we say, "set our minds at rest" without thought, there is for all of us a strong temptation to do it. Of course, thinking, praying, and seeking are great joys—the greatest of joys —to some men and women, just as climbing mountains, swimming channels, rowing races are joys to many; but even they must either keep themselves in constant training, or find a stimulus to drive them to the effort. If, in addition to this great advantage of peace without pain, agnosticism affords us the satisfaction of conscious superiority over those who are fools enough to assert that God can be known, and we can have the pleasure of displaying our deeper wisdom, the cycle of its powerful attractions is complete.

Come unto me, says the Unknown and Unknowable God, and I will give you rest, sleep, and entire self-satisfaction. What more could any man want? And yet we do want more. We want life and love, and power to heal the wounds of our humanity. And these the Unknown God has not to give. If we can shut our ears to the voice of mankind, and remain blind to their signals of distress; if we can content ourselves with the book of life before us, written in a language which we cannot read, and make no attempt to learn the language, we may indeed die gracefully and harmlessly, but we cannot hope to live. For my part I cannot do it.

> I want to live, live out, not wobble through
> My life somehow, then out into the dark,
> I must have God. This life's too dull without,
> Too dull for ought but suicide. What's Man
> To live for else? I'd murder someone just
> To see red blood. I'd drink my self blind drunk
> And see blue snakes, if I could not look up
> To see blue skies, and hear God speaking through
> The silence of the stars.

You might not, gentle reader, be so base as that. You may be much more civilized, and it may seem to you to be extravagant, but I am a primitive, vulgar man, and I would take either to drink, sensuality, or crude personal ambition. You, perhaps, would be content with more refined and decent drugs, modern novels, problem plays, scandal, bridge, mild gambling, and all the proper apparatus we clever people use to dull the pain of boredom, and the emptiness of life. You would not murder any one, but you might crush to see a murderer tried for his life, or help to absorb the ocean of evening papers which enable us to enjoy a murder without the blood and tears. I would want the blood and tears, the other turns me sick. I cannot stand the civilized methods of being savage. Savagery or sanctity I could do with, but from the modern cave man with his morbid and dishonest sensuality may the Good Lord deliver me. I must have God, a God whom I can know, and love, and live for, I must find a meaning for life.

If I am to do that I must think. How does one begin. Well, it begins with trouble in the mind. We have seen that. There is no thought without tears. "Blessed are they that mourn." "The sacrifice of God is a troubled spirit." The modern cult of cheeriness is largely due to the fact that we are deadly afraid of being sad. We want Easter without Lent. But we cannot have it. The human mind, and the human heart—and you cannot separate the one from the other—God has joined them together and no man can put them asunder.

> There's no such thing as thought which does not feel,
> If it be real thought, and not thought's ghost
> All pale and sicklied o'er with dead conventions,
> Abstract truth, which is a lie upon this
> Living, loving, suffering Truth which pleads
> And pulses in my very veins. The blue
> Blood of all beauty and the breath of life itself.

The human mind and the human heart move to truth through trouble. It does not really matter what sort of truth you seek. Bunyan faced with the problem of the soul, and Newton faced with the problem of the stars, are both alike in this; they are troubled spirits. They brood over a mass of apparently unconnected, unrelated, and meaningless facts. Bunyan mutters, "There is no health in me"; Newton mutters, "There is no sense in them." For both it is dark, and they do not know the way. Both walk at times into the dungeon of despair. The pilgrim's progress of the scientist and of the saint is made along much the same road, and it begins with a troubled brooding, and a heavy burden at the back of the heart and mind. We must all start there. Life begins in Lent. But there comes to both a supreme and splendid moment, the moment when they cry, "I see! I see!" Bunyan sees a Cross and a Man who hangs in agony upon it. Newton sees an apple falling to the ground. But into the mind of both there comes a blaze of light. For the scientist it is the formation of a great hypothesis, for the saint it is the vision of a Saviour. But the difference between those two great events is not so wide as many would suppose. They are but two different ways in which the WORD, the Person eternally expressing a reasonable purpose, reveals himself to the heart and mind of man. For both the scientist and the saint it means the coming of order into chaos. It is the perception of sense in what had been nonsense, of reason in what had seemed mad.

For both, there remains the task of walking in the light which they have seen. The scientist must apply and verify his hypothesis, the saint must work out his own salvation with fear and trembling. From the purely intellectual point of view, if there were such a thing in any but abstract questions, such as those with which pure science is concerned, from the purely intellectual point of view our faith is the great hypothesis, and our intellectual right to hold it is the same as that of the scientist to work upon and verify his hypothesis. It is impossible to exaggerate the importance of hypotheses to thought. They are the bones of science. There is no science until there is an hypothesis, a great assumption, on its trial; there is no science and no life, either. Thought and life must both begin with an act of faith. Both are born from that great moment in the pilgrim life, when a man cries out, "I see." The full meaning and application of what they see, the extension of their vision until it covers all the facts and gives a meaning to them, is in both cases the work of a lifetime. As they work new vision comes, and they may perceive that their first vision was not clear, that there is more to learn, and they must modify their early faith.

Religious people often scoff at the scientist because they say he is always changing his faith, and scientific people scoff at the religious because they never change theirs. Neither taunt is really true. It is not true that because Einstein modifies Newton therefore Newton did not see a great Truth, or that because the Darwinian hypothesis of natural selection has been found inadequate that therefore it is not true in essence. Nor is it true that religious people never change or modify their faith, they are always doing it, that is the work of the theologians. S. Augustine and Bishop Gore have both seen Christ, but what they have seen in Christ is as different in many ways as the tropics from the poles.

The Christian does not claim to know God in all the truth of His infinite Being, the claim would be manifestly absurd. Omnia abeunt in mysterium. There are depths of Truth which lie beyond us, and we bow in humility before the "mysterium tremendum" of the Father. The cheerful pantheism which is, or claims to be, on intimate and familiar terms with God, which is, so to speak, hail fellow well met with Him; the religion which does not kneel, but presumes on Love revealed in Christ, to treat God almost as an equal, is a dangerous travesty of Truth. It is a reaction from the opposite danger of the unknown and unknowable God before whose veiled face men have bowed down in fear and trembling, placating Him with servile prayers, and propitiating His irrational wrath with morbid sacrifices, and it is as far from truth as most reactions are.

The Christian claim is that God is unknown in the Infinity of the Father, well-known in the Incarnation of the Son, and infinitely knowable by the operation of the Spirit. We do not claim to know God face to face, and in His fulness; but we do claim, and claim emphatically, that through Jesus Christ, we are growing in true knowledge of Him. We do claim that whatever new knowledge of God comes to us, either as a race or as individuals, whether it comes through science or through history, will never contradict Christ. In Christ the meaning of Life is being revealed. We only see things truly as we see them all in Him. His will and His purpose are the will and the purpose of all things, and only as we use all things in accordance with His will, and for His purpose, do we use them rightly. His purpose and not our purposes. His will and not our wills. That is the essential point. If we try to take the world and mould it to our wills, and make it conform to our purposes, it will break us in pieces. It will break our hearts, and burst our brains. The world is not yours—but God's; it is not made to serve your purpose but to serve the purpose of God revealed in Christ.

That is the very essence of the Christian faith. That is the awful truth which we proclaim in the dogma of the Divinity or Deity of Christ. The reason why we reject, and must reject, the conception of the merely human Jesus, even though he be acknowledged as the greatest of all teachers, is because, if that be true, we are still without light upon the ultimate meaning and purpose of life and of the world in which we live. We have a system of ethics but not a religion, a moral code but not a vital faith. We cannot be saved by a moral code. We can only be saved as we learn to live in accordance with our real environment, like any other living creature. There is no escape from the everlasting law of selection. We must either correspond with our environment or perish, and unless we can know the true nature of our environment we cannot correspond to it. If Christ does not reveal to us the nature of reality we must find someone who does. If the Christian values are not the true values, we must discover what the true values are, or we cannot live. Our supreme hypothesis is that in Christ we have revealed to us the ultimate nature of our environment, the true meaning, value and purpose of life, and we cannot abandon it unless, and until we find a better one.

A great psychologist, Dr. Hadfield, recently expressed a doubt as to whether Christianity was the final religion.

If by that he means to question whether Christ as we see Him now, and as we interpret Him now, is the final Christ, I am sure that he is right; but if he means that we shall ever discover Goodness, Beauty, and Truth which contradict the Goodness, Beauty, and Truth revealed in that Life and Death, I am sure he is wrong.

I am convinced that, as through evolution in time, the true nature and meaning of the world in which we live is progressively revealed to us, so it will become more and more evident that we can only live in it as we conform to the Christian standard, and attain to the Christian virtues. God leads us to Christ not only through teachers, preachers, and prophets, but through life and through history. If the coming of the Kingdom of God depended solely upon the moral leaders of mankind, I would despair of it; but the purpose of God revealed in Christ is being worked out in the world, and in the history of the world.

We are being led to the Truth through the continual pressure upon us of our environment, which has *inherent in it* the purpose of God. The doctrine of the "survival of the fittest," adequately interpreted and properly understood, is ultimate truth. The "fittest" means those who most completely fit in with and correspond to their environment. But the ultimate environment of man is God "in Whom we live, and move, and have our being." Those, therefore, are "the fittest," and those alone can in the end survive, who fit in with, are in communion with, God. "This is eternal life to know Thee, the only true God, and Jesus Christ Whom Thou hast sent."

The doctrine of the survival of the fittest, which was put forward merely as a bald summary statement of ascertained fact, namely, that those animals tended to survive and propagate their species most plentifully which were best adapted to their material surroundings, has been used to lend the authority of "science" to the most perverse and ignorantly conceived philosophic ideas. It has been used to interpret human life in terms of animal life, and to depict the world as being in its ultimate nature a brutal battlefield. This teaching it is to which Christianity is utterly and irrevocably opposed. The ultimate nature of the world was revealed to man in Christ as being, not a battlefield, but a home, and its final law as being, not the law of the jungle, but the law of the family.

Let us be quite clear about the importance of that Truth. Once men really grasp the meaning of it, it will turn the world upside down or, rather, right way up. It means that if we try to use the material world as though it belonged to us, to use as we think fit, to serve our will, *every single blessing in it will become a curse.* From that terrible fact there is no escape for us either as individuals or as societies. No intellectual brilliance, or perfection of organization, no human scheming, however subtle, can enable us to subdue the world of things to our human will. We may appear to succeed for a while, but in the end we must fail and fail disastrously. We must fail because "right at the heart of the ultimate reality there was in the beginning, is now, and ever shall be a person expressing a rational purpose which we can understand," and it is this purpose which finally controls and determines our destiny because its nature is divine. We cannot know God in His fulness but He has spoken, and is speaking, and revealing to us the meaning of the world in which we live, and only as we learn to hear Him speak, and to obey His will, can we attain to life in any real sense at all. There is no such thing as success outside the will of God, either for individuals or societies.

There is no failure so ghastly as selfish and merely personal success. Whether it be the success of the business-man who gains riches and misses wealth, the success of the man in the street who wins pleasure and loses happiness, of the statesman who attains to power but fails to serve, of the beautiful woman who is universally admired but never loved—it is all failure, ugly, vulgar, piteous failure that makes not only angels, but decent human beings weep. And it is the same with nations. The weakness of the world to-day is in the Great Powers. The main reason of its poverty is its apparent wealth. Its success is its supremest failure. It has succeeded in finding the right means to attain the wrong ends. It is in the dark, and has lost its way. And yet there is light, and it grows brighter. The light shines in the darkness and the darkness has never overpowered it. The purpose and the true value of life are being progressively revealed in Christ, and as we patiently strive to find the meaning of our many-sided complex world in Him, there comes order out of chaos, sense out of nonsense, sanity out of madness.

If we will patiently brood over the tangled, confused, and tragic maze of facts which make up human history and experience, there will come the moment when we cry, " I see," and there will swim into our vision the master fact of Christ. We shall progressively perceive that He is the door by which we enter into the palace of Truth, as we faithfully apply the great hypothesis to the problems, personal and social, that baffle and perplex us. But we must apply it boldly and universally, we must not allow any part of our lives to remain unexamined and uncriticised in the light of it. The very essence of the hypothesis is in its universality, it either applies to everything or to nothing. If we apply it only to certain sections or departments of life we do not apply it at all. 'Now are we the children of God, it does not yet appear what we shall be—but we know that when He shall appear, we shall be like Him, for we shall see Him as He is.' God has spoken and is speaking, and though His WORD does not reveal the whole of His infinite Mind, yet He is Truth ; and as we apply and act upon the Truth we have, we gain more and more, until at last we come to know even as we are known. This is the Christian Faith.

Since so it is, and in that face for me,
The final beauty burns to birth,
And all things fair in heaven and earth
Are summed and centred in a mystery
Of Loveliness
Beyond compare,
How could my soul do less
Than worship Him as Saviour and as God !
Dim though my vision be
Yet that faint gleam my faith can see,
Of Christ, is brighter than the sun,
Without it all the world is bare

And barren as a winter's day,
Whose cold grey
Hours run,
From dark to dark,
Without a dawn or sunset sky
To tell the Truth that Love is there
Through all.
Without it pleasures fade and fall,
As petals from a rotting rose,
To leave the thorns behind;
Without it I am blind,
And, through a wilderness of woes,
Go blindly blundering on to death,
And nothingness at last,
Which is damnation of the soul.

CHAPTER III

All things through Him came into being, and apart from Him not a single thing came into being which is of the nature of reality.

S. JOHN i. 3.

THE statement of the great Christian hypothesis of life proceeds with a further vigorous emphasis upon its universality. Nothing which is of the nature of reality lies outside its scope, absolutely nothing. Everything which claims to possess significance or reality apart from the eternal purpose of God expressed in Christ is an imposture and a lie. In Him, and in Him alone, all things consist, as S. Paul puts it.

It is precisely to this universal claim of the Christian faith, that our modern way of thought and life is most obviously opposed. There are few who would not allow that religion ought to play a part in life, but most men would deny that it is meant to dominate the whole of it. Yet it destroys the very nature of religion to make it a department of life and thought. Religion is, from the intellectual point of view, an hypothesis as to the meaning of the whole universe, and from the moral and spiritual point of view a life based in every department of it upon that hypothesis. We cannot divide the world into departments without dividing ourselves, and to divide the human personality is to destroy it. That is what we are doing. Destroying our souls by dividing our lives, and it is from that destruction that our religion ought to save us.

There are many reasons why this division of life into watertight compartments is a specially strong temptation to us in these latter days. It is a tragedy which arises directly from a triumph. There has been a modern triumph, and it is shallow thinking to belittle or deny it. The great and unparalleled advance of Science in the last century is one of the most dramatic and awe-inspiring events in human history. It is all very well for Disraeli to sneer at it, but his sneer is a judgment upon himself, rather than upon the great revolution in human affairs which he was blind enough to despise. The invention of the steam locomotive and the coming into the world of mechanical power, was probably the most epoch-making event in time, if we except the emergence of mind from matter, and the birth of Jesus Christ. It is as an event of enormous moral and spiritual significance, and the tragedy of our times lies in the fact that we have not realized that significance in Christ, and as part of the eternal purpose of God.

We have regarded it as what we call a purely secular event. No one would deny its immense importance from the economic, industrial, political, and social standpoint, but what on earth has it got to do with God or with religion? That is the typical outlook of the modern mind, all divided up into sections which are never joined into a whole. God made mountains, stars, and rivers, but man made machines. God made the country, man made the town. We divide the world between us, God and I, which often means in practice I and God. There is the horror of it, it is such rank impertinence, such ridiculous and insufferable pride, all the more insufferable because it is mostly unconscious. Let us frankly acknowledge that it has arisen partly in consequence of the power of false religion. Science had to fight religion for the right to seek after Truth. It has its saints and martyrs from Galileo downwards. They are every whit as much God's Saints and Martyrs as S. Stephen or S. Paul. The spectacle of Galileo sitting up in prison repeating the seven penitential Psalms, because he dared to differ from Moses and the theologians, and of poor Descartes burning his book "On the World" in case he got into trouble too, must have made the angels weep, if it did not make them laugh.

That nonsense was also the result of pride. Men suffered from what Hilary of Tours calls "irreligiosa solicitudo pro Deo," a blasphemous anxiety to do God's work for Him. They had to protect God's Truth because He could not look after it Himself. We still suffer from that form of pride and of fear. There are still men who would persecute their political and theological opponents if they could.

But the modern form of pride, which finds expression in secularism, and the division of life into departments, has other roots as well as that of opposition to ignorance and superstition. It arises partly from the nature of the scientific method itself, which, as the field of human knowledge widens, makes more and more specialized study inevitable, and so tends to produce a specialized mind, blind to certain aspects of the truth, and is, moreover, in itself a method of abstraction, taking a group of phenomena out of their setting in reality, and examining them apart from their intricate relations to the rest of the universe. Thus the science of anatomy is bound to treat the human body apart from the mind, as a thing in itself, although a body apart from a mind of some sort is nothing but a potential mass of putrefaction. But still more the curse of pride is due to the fact that the men who made the great discoveries, and, under God, bestowed upon mankind the mighty powers of which he is possessed, were not the men who used them, nor had they power to decree the purposes for which they should be used.

It is often said, and still more often assumed in thought, that man has conquered nature and subdued her to his will. But the great men to whom we owe our present powers know how false a way of thinking this is. *Man has not conquered, he has learned to obey.* Those who have been trained to divest their minds of pride and prejudice, and with untiring and persistent patience to watch, to ponder, and observe, striving to see things always as they are, in order to discover the law of their being, retain a wholesome awe and reverence for the great objective reality that faces them. They know that what they must attain to is not conquest but communion, they seek not to subdue but to understand and obey. Einstein has said of Max Planck, the physicist: "The emotional condition which fits him for his task is akin to that of a devotee or a lover." The very essence of a truly scientific mind is not pride of power but a passionate humility. Pride and cock-sureness are characteristic, not of the scientist, but of the hack thinkers, teachers, and traders who impart or assist in exploiting the discoveries of other men greater than themselves. It is to this host of lesser minds and meaner souls that we chiefly owe our modern secularism. They swarm like vultures round any new gift God bestows upon mankind, seeing in it only power for themselves. They have no reverence or respect for nature. They have only one question to ask about any fresh discovery: "Will it pay? Is there money in it?" They do not think of the new gift as a gift given for a purpose to mankind, they regard it as a lucky chance that has happened for themselves. That is the deadly danger of scientific advance. It takes a fine mind to make a discovery, but any fool, or cunning knave, can use it for his own ends. Thus Prof. Soddy talks with justice of "The treatment habitually accorded in this country to the poor discoverer, and inventor, preyed upon by rascals of every description who flourish under the protective majesty of the law, and in the grip of a commercialism that deems it the highest wisdom not to pay for anything it can get by any other means!

It is to this host of primitive and animal-minded exploiters that we mainly owe our modern secular world, which claims for itself significance and reality, outside of and apart from the purpose of God in Christ, and proclaims for itself a law which contradicts the moral law. It is to them we owe the fact that the century of science thought mainly in terms of Will, and of material power, rather than in terms of Truth. Men were, and are still, drunk with power. They thought of the world as a dead material thing which they could mould and fashion into any shape they pleased. They did not perceive any worthy purpose in life; they were too intent on making it serve their own shortsighted and instinctive purposes. They only wanted to use things, and not to worry about what was their proper use. Utilitarianism was their characteristic mode of thought. They did not ask themselves so much "What does this mean ? " as " What use is it to me ? " Man was the measure of all things.

Religious people, for the most part, assented to the spirit of their time, allowing their religion to become divorced from everyday life, and failing to find any religious significance in the vast revolution taking place before their eyes. To them also this was obviously man's doing, not God's. It was a purely secular business without any bearing on the spiritual life of man. The results of this essentially irreligious and unthinking attitude, which still persists and is powerful to-day, have been literally disastrous. It has meant that every fresh blessing from God has been turned into a curse, and every new power has become a source of weakness. The machine has become a master rather than a servant. It is not machines that serve men, but millions of men that serve machines, and become themselves mechanical. The whole world has grown into a mechanical device which runs or fails to run according to laws of its own—and whether it runs or fails to run, grinds out misery for millions. It went on grinding faster and faster until it reached a ghastly climax, and we stood and looked upon the crowning blasphemy, a great modern gun in action, discharging poison gas ; a monster embodying within itself a whole century of exact and beautiful knowledge, and using it for a purpose that would make a decent savage blush with shame, while from the altars on both sides passionate prayers went up to a tribal God of War for victory in arms. It is a shameful memory. Shameful not merely because it was barbarous, but because it was blasphemous, a denial of the omnipresence of God, a rejection of the great hypothesis, " Through Him all things came into being and apart from Him not a single thing came into being which is of the nature of reality." It is as though we had tied Christ to our cursed guns and made him look on while we butchered and dishonoured his children. It is this denial of Christ which is shouted at us from every corner of our modern world. Everywhere we are surrounded by the sacraments of our sin, the outward and visible signs of our inward and spiritual disgrace. God gave us stones wherewith to build the new Jerusalem, and we turned out Glasgow, Birmingham, Calcutta, and Tokio. Those who have knowledge can understand what those names stand for in terms of human souls.

And yet that is not the whole picture, thank God, if it were, I could not believe that there was a God to thank. God is not mocked. His Will works on, in spite of all, His purpose still prevails. The purpose which is immanent and inherent in the great new powers is being wrought out. Those who have eyes to see can see it, and the first need of our time is for seers, men and women with vision. God has overruled our folly, and made even the wrath of man to serve Him. He has flatly contradicted our plans, and destroyed our purposes making them serve His own. The mills of God grind slowly, but they grind exceeding small. The work of countless millions of men trying to use God's gifts to serve themselves, and make themselves independent and self-sufficient, independent of God and of their fellow-men; the ideal of independent individuals, independent classes, independent sovereign nations, which was the dominant ideal of the age of change, has been overruled and has produced a world in which independence is revealed, as being not merely a philosophical absurdity, but a practical impossibility, a world in which interdependence, universal interdependence, is the most obvious and self-evident fact of life. Thus the essential nature of the world in which we live, has, in spite of our blundering, our blindness, and our sin, progressively revealed itself in time, and it is made plain that we cannot live in it unless we conform to the Christian standard, and attain to the Christian virtues. The new environment, which is the due development of the old, but is nevertheless new, unparalleled and unprecedented in the history of man, demands imperatively as a response, that new life which came into the world with Jesus Christ.

We did not propose for ourselves this new creation, we never intended it, so far as we intended anything, it was the exact opposite we sought, and are still seeking; but there's a divinity that shapes our ends, rough hew them how we will, and God has made of the world one body, which, if it is to live at all, must learn to live exactly in the manner in which S. Paul describes the life of the Church "closely joined and knit together by the contact of every part with the source of its life, deriving its power to grow in proportion to the vigour of each individual part; and so being built up in a spirit of Love."

There are just two alternatives that face the world to-day, either that life or agony and death. The enormous increase in population, and the conquest of space and time by increased rapidity of communication, both of which are only rendered possible by a continual division and subdivision of labour, have locked and bound us all into a material unity of universal interdependence from which we cannot escape, and which we must therefore either acknowledge and respond to in spirit or perish. Our environment constitutes a self-evident moral and spiritual challenge. We must either adapt ourselves to this intensely complex and delicate network of human relationships, which our environment imposes upon us as a necessity, or face the perpetual and inevitable alternative of death, which has faced all living things ever since the world began. That is no "high falutin" extravagant theory, but the plainest and most indisputable fact in the world of to-day. It is the Lord's doing and is marvellous in the eyes of those who see. Once more we return to the prophetic view of life, and see it all as a matter of life and death, a crisis, a great choice which we must make now or never. And this choice comes to every individual soul, and his salvation here and hereafter depends upon how he answers to the call. *The fate of the world depends upon the social responsibility of the individual, and his power and willingness to bear it.* It is in form and content a social responsibility, arising out of the new relationship with our fellow-men and women into which the working out of God's purpose has brought us, but it can only be borne by individuals in the last analysis. Corporate action we must take, but right corporate action cannot be taken except as individuals hear the call and answer, acting as personalities responsible to God for their actions. The question of all questions is whether the ordinary individual man can bear the enormous burden of personal responsibility which the new world imposes upon him. At present it seems impossible. The ordinary man is bewildered and perplexed, trying to shift and shirk the responsibility, and to put his trust in mass movements and organizations. Mass movement and organization we must have; those who despise and decry them are mostly people who do not want to bear the moral responsibilities which they impose upon them, but desire what they call freedom, power to express themselves, independence of this crawling crowding mass of humanity, which they gratuitously assume is inferior to themselves. If they are clever enough, and forceful enough, they can still gain for themselves, and maintain under the protection of the law, a certain measure of this freedom, living in the world as if it were made for their special benefit, but their lives are a living, or, rather, rapidly dying lie.

The outcry against organization and rational regulation of our corporate life is largely the refuge of moral cowards from the insistent call of God. But mass movement and organization can themselves be used as a refuge from that call, they can be used to save the individual from the painful duties of thought and righteous action, and, when they are so used, they constitute the most terrible menace to which we are exposed. When an organization or mass movement becomes an end in itself, and mere loyalty to it is regarded as the highest duty, whether it be a nation, a class, a party, or a Church the result is the moral and spiritual degradation of the individual soul. Churches, nations, classes, parties, unions of a hundred different kinds, are necessary and inevitable, it is worse than useless to object to them, but they will be good or bad, constructive or destructive, *exactly in proportion as they increase or decrease the sense of personal responsibility in the hearts and minds of the individuals composing them.* The fate of a complex civilization ultimately depends upon the mental and moral quality of the individuals who bear it.

It is, therefore, not merely necessary that we should be as good, individually, as our fathers; we must be very much better. Advancing civilization with every step of progress makes greater and greater mental and moral demands upon its bearers. This is the will of God, the method, a stern and terrible method, by which He educates His children.

There are many who declare that the method is not divine but devilish, that it is a scandalously cruel and manifestly ineffective method to which man has no power to respond. They regard civilization, and its moral complexity, as a curse, an invention of the devil, or the result of accident, which will inevitably collapse, leaving men to return to the simple life which they are really capable of living. To them modern problems, politics, industry, economics, are purely secular still, they have nothing to do with pure religion, and the simple Gospel of eternal life. They do not want them brought into Church or into prayers; they want to have one place upon earth where they will never hear a word about war, wages, housing, unemployment, and all the rest of it. They have my sympathy, but it will not do. It is only another way of evading responsibility, and refusing the call of God to come up higher. The religion they want would not be religion at all; it would be a species of entertainment and relaxation. That is, what much of our religion is, a substitute for the picture-show. We come because we like the service, the music, the preacher, the atmosphere of the place. It soothes us with its sanctity and enables us to sleep and dream. But this is not religion. These churches are not churches, they are little herds of like-minded people snuggling up to one another for comfort and warmth as animals do. They have their yelps and yowls just like the beasts, their party shibboleths, and common cant, but the life of God is not in them—the mark of the beast is upon them. Their unity does not depend upon their response to the call of God, but upon the primitive instinct of the herd, whereby birds of a feather flock together—Protestant birds and Catholic birds, High Church, Low Church, Free Church birds, but all birds obeying an impulse, not men that hear a call. The world is full of flocks and herds, but what it needs is a society, and a society only exists as every member of it is consciously and intelligently responsive to the call of a higher purpose, and obedient to a higher Will

It is this universal Society which the environment of modern civilization presses upon us perpetually as an imperative necessity, as the only way by which we can attain that harmony with our environment which is life. God calls us through His gifts to follow the more excellent way of Love, which is the only way of Life. The very essence of religion is to give to these new relationships their true moral and spiritual meaning, to link up our daily work with our daily worship, our common duties with our common faith. Civilization demands the Christian virtues, and cannot continue to exist without a greater and greater measure of them in every individual man and woman. It is instinct in every part with the Presence of that 'Person expressing a reasonable purpose through Whom all things came into being, and apart from Whom not a single thing came into being which is of the nature of reality.' Therefore, its call is the call of Christ.

The thunder of our modern traffic, the manifold complexity of our modern industry, the intricate workings of modern economics and finance repeat, and give new force and meaning to the pleading of S. Paul for His Lord. "I therefore the prisoner of the Lord beseech you that ye walk worthy of the call, wherewith ye are called; humble, for the world is God's not yours; meek, for every human being with whom you are brought into contact is a soul for whom Christ died, a sacred personality, and you have no right to use Him for yourself; patient, for the task is tremendous amd men are frail; forbearing one another in Love, for violence is useless, and domination does not help; endeavouring to keep in the bond of Peace the unity bestowed by the spirit of Christ, the only unity which in the end can hold. There is but one Body, lift up your eyes and look upon it, this new world Body that I have made, wrought of iron and of steel, whirling on its multitude of wheels within wheels, jointed with a million miles of rail, with its wire nerves that tremble to the touch of thought, its very ether vibrant with reasonable speech. Sweat and blood, the tears and terror of mankind, the travail of the soul of God are in it—but it is done. There is but one Body, and there must be but one

Spirit. If that body is to live it can only live in Him through Whom it was created—the eternal WORD of God; through Whom all things were made, and without Whom not a single thing was made which has been made. So through the thunder of our world machine there comes a human voice, saying:

O heart I made, a heart beats here for thee,
Face my hands fashioned see it in Myself,
Thou hast no power nor mayst conceive of mine,
But Love I gave Thee with myself to Love,
And thou must Love me who have died for Thee.

CHAPTER IV

In Him was Life,
And the life was the light of men,
And the light shines in the darkness,
And the darkness cannot overcome it.

S. JOHN i, 4, 5.

STILL the cry of the prisoned spirit, the agonizing effort to express the inexpressible, the signals of a man who has seen more than he can say. Life, Light, Darkness, great elemental metaphors which God Himself must in the end interpret to the soul. There was life before there was light. Darkness is the tragic unexplained and inexplicable background of it all. It is the drama of a dawn that has not found as yet the glory of the perfect day. Before Man there was life but no light. There was sensation but no intelligence. That is the miracle of man. In him we see mere sensation passing into intelligence. Yet the life of mere sensation persists, it clouds but cannot destroy intelligence. " The Light shines in the darkness, and the darkness cannot overcome it."

Let us think of vision and what it means. Let us think of Browning's poems in the claws of a chimpanzee. There is sensual sight keener and more powerful than our own. He sees the book, claws at it, smells it, tries to eat it, tears it into pieces and throws it away. Life but no light, sensation but no intelligence. You behaved like that when you were a baby. The whole world once behaved like that before the light dawned. There was once life, but no light.

Millions and millions of living creatures seeing, hearing, smelling, touching, breeding, but not understanding. Darkness, which is not darkness to them because they have no light.

Then think of Browning's Poems in the hands of a boy of ten, or a prosperous but unenlightened stockbroker of forty. He sees it, he can read it, he can understand the relation of the printed symbols to one another, he can put them together and make with his lips the sounds they stand for. There is intellectual perception. But it does not interest him, he is bored with it. The boy will use it as a stand to put his toy steam engine on; the man to prop up the leg of a wobbly table that he writes business letters on. 'The light shines in the darkness, and the darkness cannot overcome it.' Both have an uneasy feeling that the book was meant for something else.

Now think of Browning's Poems in the hands of one who knows. There he sits rapt and still, and very happy, his body upon the earth, his soul in another world.

> It is not what man Does which exalts him, but what man would do!
> See the King—I would help him but cannot, the wishes fall through.
> Could I wrestle to raise him from sorrow, grow poor to enrich,
> To fill up his life starve my own out, I would—knowing which
> I know that my service is perfect. Oh, speak through me now!
> Would I suffer for him that I love? So wouldst Thou. So wilt Thou!
> So shall crown Thee the topmost, ineffablest, uttermost crown—
> And Thy Love fill infinitude wholly, nor leave up nor down
> One spot for the creature to stand in! It is by no breath,
> Turn of eye, wave of hand, that Salvation joins issue with Death!
> As Thy Love is discovered almighty, almighty be proved
> Thy power, that exists with and for it, of being Beloved!
> He who did most, shall bear most; the strongest shall stand the most weak.
> 'Tis the weakness in strength that I cry for! my flesh that I seek
> In the Godhead! I seek and find it. O Saul, it shall be
> A Face like my face that receives thee: a Man like to Me.

Thou shalt love and be loved by for ever! A Hand like this hand
Shall throw open the gates of new Life to thee! See the Christ stand!

He sees with the sensual sight of the animal, with the intellectual perception of the boy or the broker, but both are crowned and completed in the spiritual vision of the seer. He sees through the material page, and through the ordered symbolic sounds, the world of eternal values, the spiritual world of Beauty, Truth, and Goodness, the light of which the printed poem is the shadow. Yet he knows that he sees imperfectly, there is darkness still; but the light shines in the darkness, and the darkness, O, thank God, the darkness cannot overcome it.* Well, all the world is God's poem, it is created through the WORD, and there is, therefore, a reason, a purpose, a sublime meaning in it. But, before that meaning can be grasped by men, life must pass into light, sensation must grow through intelligence into spiritual vision. The history of the living world from the protoplasm to the Christ, and of every

* 'The light shines in the darkness, and the darkness cannot overcome it.' Can't it? Can't it? you say. It can. It does. Millions live and die in the darkness. There is a glimmer of light in childhood while innocency lives on ignorance; then it flickers, fades, and dies, and men go out into the dark. What is the good of your wretched Christian optimism when you know it is not true. Don't you know that men die in the dark? I do; I do. I cannot explain it. I cannot explain the darkness. I can only defy and seek to destroy it in the power of the light, and I know that in some measure it can be destroyed. I do not know anything about it. I cannot say why or whence it comes. I only know that God did not make it. I know that the Word is not in it, nor is it in the Word. There is no reason and no purpose in it. Perhaps that is why it cannot be explained. You cannot reason about the unreasonable or explain the irrational. If you can make sense out of nonsense it never was nonsense. Evil is nonsense. It is irrational and mad. That is the very essence of it. It has no ultimate objective existence because it was not made by God through the Word, through Whom all things came into being, and apart from Whom not one single thing came into being which is of the nature of reality. Evil has no substance because it has no absolute value. If you bring it down to tin-tacks you can put that this way. If you submit to evil you are wasting your time. It is a fraud. Get rid of it quick. As long as you believe in it it will enslave you, but where there is light there is liberty.

individual soul, which, in itself, recapitulates the story of the race, is the story of that passage from mere sensation to spiritual vision, from the vision of things, to the vision of the relation of things in time, to the vision of the value of things in eternity.

There is no sense or meaning in the world as seen by sensual sight nor as seen by mere intellectual perception. So long as we live on the level of the senses, and the material intellect, we can never discern any meaning in life that will stand the test of time or the self-destructive power of the critical faculty. Mere intellect can do nothing but commit suicide. We cannot think in the light and live in the dark or dim twilight. The only world we can know is the world in which we live, which depends upon the kind of sight we have. We cannot think about or reason from any other world than that of our own experience. Yet there is a real world apart from our idea of it, there is an objective reality other than ourselves. There is a real poem written by God Himself, and there are a million million versions of it, in a million million minds, some come near to the poem itself, some are the wildest caricatures of it. No one can read the real poem unless he is in spiritual communion with the poet, who is God. Two men argue about the meaning of the world, and neither can convince the other, because they live in different worlds. Each is talking about the world of his own experience, and their experiences are utterly different. Each of us builds his own world out of the stimuli to which he responds, the things, that is, to which he attends. It is impossible for us to attend to a hundredth part of the things that claim our attention in the course of a single day, we are always, consciously or unconsciously, selecting what we shall see and what we shall hear. We attend only to what interests us, and so we see andfear mostly what we desire to see and hear.

There is a story told of an old maiden lady who was very deaf. She went out for a walk one morning in the spring, accompanied by her sister. As they passed over a railway cutting, an express train dashed with a shriek into a tunnel, and Aunt Jane turned to her sister and said, with a beaming smile: " My dear, I am sure I heard a lark sing." There is humour and pathos in that. All morning that lark had been singing in her soul, and she interpreted the sound that reached her ears according to her heart's desire. We all do the same. We cannot help it. All day long our eyes and ears are assailed by a million sights and sounds, and we interpret them, and select from them, according to our heart's desire. We are all of us really stronger in the heart than in the head. Pure reason is a fiction or abstraction.

The great mistake which nineteenth-century thinkers made was their calm assumption that men are born rational beings. They taught that, whereas animals were wholly impulsive and instinctive creatures, men were wholly rational. From this absurdly optimistic position experience and research combine to rout us utterly. Experience first, for if the history of the last ten years in Europe is to be read as the story of purely rational beings, then either the word rational loses its meaning, or history becomes an intolerable enigma. We have behaved like brute beasts. Mr. Bertrand Russell tells sad truth when he says that we might perchance attain to Peace and turn the Industrial Revolution from a curse into a blessing, if politics could become rational, but at present there is not the slightest sign of a change in that direction. What is called political reality is composed of passion and impulse for the most part, with thought, at best, as light just breaking through; very faint and dim as yet. 'The darkness cannot overcome it,' is still an act of faith rather than a statement of realized fact; it is a Truth discerned and discernible only by spiritual vision, not by intellectual perception. Rationality is not a natural inheritance, but a supernatural achievement; it comes from above and not below.

Psychological research comes in to confirm experience, and enables us to see the reason of it. It makes quite clear the fact that our kinship with the animals, which Darwin demonstrated in the make-up of our bodies, must be admitted as extending further to the make-up of our minds. Not only do I look like a monkey, a fact which is sadly evident on the face of it, but I frequently behave like one. And so, gentle reader, however gentle and refined you be, so do you. The cynic says that women are cats, and men are dogs. Pause and ask yourself how often in the past twelve months that has been true of you. How often have you snarled and spit, and scratched, and bitten your fellows in the back, metaphorically of course, in thought and word, though not, perhaps, in deed. It would make our confessions more real sometimes if we confessed that we had behaved like cats and dogs, rather than that we were miserable sinners. There is a dignity we don't deserve about a miserable sinner. Really, we have been just ugly beasts; monkeys with a human brain. The most awful thing the mind can conceive is a gorilla with a Napoleonic intellect. It is God's mercy that we sinners are so often fools.

We are born with a very powerful set of impulses and instincts which we share with the animals, and in them lie, to a large extent, the driving forces of our personalities.

As Dr. William McDougall puts it: "We may say then that directly or indirectly the instincts are the prime movers of all human activity; by the conative or impulsive force of some instinct (or of some habit derived from an instinct) every train of thought, however cold and passionless it may seem to be, is borne along towards its end, and every bodily activity is initiated and sustained. The instinctive impulses determine the end of all activities, and supply the driving power by which all mental activities are sustained; and all the complex intellectual apparatus of the most highly developed mind is but a means towards those ends, is but the instrument by which those impulses seek their satisfactions, while pressure and pain do but serve to guide them in their choice of means. Take away these instinctive dispositions with their powerful impulses, and the organism would become incapable of activity of any kind; it would lie inert and motionless like a wonderful clockwork whose mainspring had been removed, or a steam engine whose fires had been drawn. These impulses are the mental forces that maintain and shape the life of individuals and societies, and in them we are confronted with the central mystery of life, and mind, and will."

That could not be better put. We are largely creatures of impulse, of sensation without intelligence, largely but not wholly. The discovery of the leading part that impulse plays in the determination of our conduct, and the formation of our judgments, has led to a violent swing of the pendulum, a swing from rationalism to irrationalism, from the uncritical worship to the uncritical contempt of reason. That will not do. We are largely animal, but we are not animals. An animal is born in a natural state of internal harmony—men are not; *they have to attain to and achieve internal harmony.* Between the lowest man and the highest animal there is a great gulf fixed, a gulf immeasurably greater than that which exists between the highest and the lowest kind of man. An animal follows its impulses blindly, using what rudimentary intelligence it possesses, merely to enable it to satisfy its instinctive desires, and it lives thus in health and contentment. A man cannot do that; if he tries to do it, he is led neither to health nor to harmony, but to hell, in the truest sense of the word. That is the fallacy of the gospel of "self-expression," before you have attained a self to express. If "self-expression" merely means the undisciplined satisfaction of disordered and unharmonized impulse, it can only, and will inevitably, lead you not to health and happiness, but to the death and disintegration of the personality, which is damnation. Let there be no mistake about that. Anyone who tells you that the way out of your moral conflicts is to give free rein to your desires, is either a knave or the most ignorant and dangerous kind of fool. If he cloaks his advice under the cant of modern psychology it is proof positive that he does not know B from a bull's foot about it.

We must achieve a self to express; we must attain to an internal harmony. And, although we are not borne with the harmony ready-made, we are born with an immensely powerful impulse to achieve it. The hall-mark of humanity is the urge to make a unity, a harmony of ourselves. This urge, which is, of course, essentially one, we can conveniently dissect for purposes of thought into two main manifestations, reason and religion. We are not born either rational or holy but we are born reasoning and religious. The impulse to reason is the urge to make a harmony or unity of our experience. It is always the perception of a discord that makes us think, the 'pain in the mind' of which we have already spoken. But the effort of our reason to make a harmony of experience will always be futile and unavailing, so long as the impulses and passions (which naturally determine our interests, and therefore determine the nature of our experience, which is built out of the things to which we attend because they interest us), are themselves unharmonized and disordered. We cannot have an orderly mind with an undisciplined and chaotic heart. There is, therefore, in us an urge to unify our desire nature also, and this urge is the raw material of religion.

From the subjective standpoint, that is, viewed from the inside, a man's religion is his ruling passion. Man is naturally addicted to ruling passions, to going " crazy " about things, as we say. Animals don't do it. Cows don't go crazy about chewing their cud, nor monkeys about cracking nuts or climbing trees, but there is hardly anything from the Love of God to gambling and golf about which men do not tend to go "crazy." Millions of men count themselves sane because they invariably suffer from the proper popular madness. We still use a religious word for this strange human propensity we call it " enthusiasm," a word which implies that men are " inspired by " or " possessed by " a God. We even say, with an insight greater than we know, " he makes a regular religion of it," and " it " may be anything—sport, sexual adventure, money-making, social position, etc., *ad infinitum.* But if you examine human enthusiasms, in all their variety, you will discover that they all centre around some powerful primitive instinct, or complex of instincts—sport round self-assertion and self-display, sexual adventure round sex, acquisition and self-assertion, money-making round acquisitiveness and self-assertion, social position round self-assertion and the herd instinct, and so on through an endless cycle of permutations and combinations all made of the same primitive elements.

Examine yourself and see if that is not true of you. Ask what interests you and why ? See that man in the corner of the railway carriage glued to a book, unconscious of time. What holds him ? Ten to one it is a romance (sex), a detective story (curiosity), a battle or race or prize fight (pugnacity), a great career (self-assertion). The second or third-rate artist who works for money, if he knows his job, goes straight for your animal instincts and plays on them. It is one of the most paying jobs in the world at present, and one of the most pernicious. The advertisers use the power of sex to sell soap, cigarettes, boots, baby linen, and vacuum cleaners. They know you often better than you know yourself. That is how they make their money.

A boy grows up through a series of enthusiasms which group themselves around his natural impulses as they develop, and these enthusiasms, which determine his interests, tend to determine the experience out of which his reason has to make a harmony if he is to find health and peace. Religious growth and education, in their broadest sense, are the right development and direction of enthusiasm. But too often it is wrongly directed and badly developed. The desire nature of the boy or girl never attains to any sort of synthesis and harmony. He never really grows up. He then either suffers from one false religion after another, or gets one false one and sticks to it, or progressively loses his religious faculty altogether, and becomes gradually incapable of enthusiasm of any sort. The last state is in many ways the worst of all. It generally disguises some secret, unacknowledged, and more or less disreputable enthusiasm probably connected with sex or some odd phantasy of the self, a pose of some sort or other ; their name is legion. Many of those who scoff at religious devotion are devoted to the point of idiocy to things less sane and less reputable, probably themselves. You cannot get rid of religion by denying God, any more than you can get rid of Sex by refusing to marry. It only breaks out in another and probably less respectable place—some form of self-adoration. We are all desperately liable to hypocrisy, play-acting with ourselves as hero or heroine. Where absence of enthusiasm does not disguise a pose, a phantasy, or secret enthusiasm, it means that the man has ceased to live and begun to die more or less rapidly.

In any case, where he has not attained to some synthesis and harmony of impulse, has not achieved any adequate an worthy enthusiasm which harmonizes his desire nature, he will continue to reason without ever becoming rational in the true sense of that word. His reason will continue the effort to build up a harmonious world out of a discordant and meaningless experience, and will continually fail, until he gives it up and begins to die more or less under protest. Thousands of so-called living people are just more or less rabid Protestants against death. They refuse to grow old, they cannot remain young; and so they become artificial antique. Sex centred, self-centred, money-centred, anything and everything but God-centred anomalies; elderly infantile misfits that wander round in worlds unrealized. That, as far as I can see, is what it means to be damned or at any rate in process of damnation.

There is a very popular mistrust of enthusiasm which leads people to imagine that it is always and inevitably opposed to rationality. It is commonest among what are called practical people—men and women who are counted sane because their form of madness is peculiarly prevalent at the time, and they use all the fashionable drugs to make it tolerable. It includes all those hard-headed men who are convinced that the proper purpose of life is to make a living; which is manifestly a lunatic notion if one stops to think. The idea is that the way to attain rationality is to be enthusiastic about nothing, to divest the mind of emotion altogether, and so become purely rational. You therefore abandon religion, which is, as we have seen, a developed and directed enthusiasm. The phrase to conjure with among such is scientific, "the scientific attitude," "the scientific mind." This arises from the fact that success in the abstract sciences has been attained partly by divesting the mind, so far as possible, of all emotion, and approaching the subject in a spirit of detachment. And it is assumed that because this is possible in the realm of abstract science, it is therefore possible in the realm of concrete life. But there lies the fallacy. It is possible to be detached and emotionless about the binomial theorem because nobody, but the really rational enthusiast for pure Truth who discovered it, and the few who really understand it, care a hang whether it is true or not. It is possible to be detached about somebody else's banking account, and to treat it as a matter of pure mathematics, but it is not so easy with our own. But abstract questions are not the real questions of life; they are not the principal constituents of our experience, the "live issues" about which it is most imperative that we should be rational. We have to become rational about questions involving the relations between our children and other people's children (political questions), our country and other people's countries (international questions), our pockets and other people's pockets (economic questions), our pride and other people's pride (personal questions), questions, that is, in which, by their very nature powerful primitive impulses are of necessity involved. When we pretend that we approach these live issues in a purely detached frame of mind, divested of all emotion, we indulge in puerile self-deception—conscious or unconscious. What we really do is to use our reason to justify and rationalize our passions and our prejudices, and the keener our intellect is the more efficiently does it serve their purposes. It is a stupid man, indeed, who cannot invent logical justifications for any policy or course of action which flatters his pride or fills his pocket. This is the twilight mind of the boy of ten or the broker of forty, who, up to a point, can make anything true that he desires to be true. It is also, in a subtler form, the academic mind, which attains to reason by forsaking life, and worshipping a theory, a theory which is very often a thin and inadequate disguise for the impulse of self-assertion. The peculiar vice of second-rate scholars is self-conceit. This is the material intellect, the intellect which still serves the impulses, however they may be disguised.

The primitive impulses cannot be destroyed or ignored, they must be harmonized and unified, centred in one worthy and dominant desire, which is your religion. There is, therefore, no way to rationality, in the true sense, except through religion. Religion and rationality are two aspects of one thing, the one cannot really exist without the other. Religion, of course, is not necessarily a good thing. It may be, and often is, the vilest and most contemptible of all things; it entirely depends, for its worth or worthlessness, upon its object. "Tantum religio potuit suadere malorum" (See Thou to what vile deeds religion draweth men) is a great truth. In the name of religion, men have done the most repulsive and disgusting deeds, and done them with a rampant and reckless certainty that they were right, which made them impervious to reason or argument.

Just because true religion is the best, false religion is the worst of all things. "Corruptio optimi pessima." That is why it is the very crown and climax of shallow-thinking cant to say that it does not matter what you believe. It is the one thing in the world that does matter Literally everything depends upon it as far as you and your worth to God and man is concerned. To say that it does not matter is to assert that, so long as you centre your whole life round someone or something, it does not matter in the least what it is. The enthusiastic and devoted miser is as good as the devoted and enthusiastic minister; the devout hunter of honours, as sane as the devout healer of men. That is manifestly absurd. Religion is a dangerous thing. It is mental dynamite which can either blow you to heaven or drive you to hell.

There is only one way of becoming rational on "live issues," questions in which by their very nature primitive impulses and passions are involved, and that is by the possession of one supreme and worthy passion which can dominate and direct, without destroying, your other passions, one supreme and worthy enthusiasm which can include and yet control all lesser enthusiasms. This is your religion, your passion for God. You cannot be sane unless you are crazy about Christ and The WORD. You are then mad upon the highest form of sanity. Through the power of this passion, if it be pure and strong, you pass from sensual sight, through intellectual perception, to spiritual vision, and are able to discern the true meaning of life, reading God's poem with a heart in full sympathy with the poet, and so more and more the light shines in the darkness, and the darkness tends to die away. In the power of the sublime white hot enthusiasm which is true religion, the lower passions are lifted up, sublimated as the psychologists say. Your interest, and therefore your attention, are directed more and more to the Good, the Beautiful, and the True. Your experience improves in quality, as you see things you never saw, and hear things you never heard, not that they were not there to see and hear, but you were blind and deaf, because you were not interested. Now the task of your reason becomes a possible one, your experience becomes a unity with a meaning, you discern the purpose and value of life, and learn to cry with utter conviction, "In the beginning was the Word," there is reason at the heart of things. Then you become rational about your children and other people's children, because they are all God's children, your country and other countries because they are God's countries, your pocket and other people's pockets because all good things are of God to be held in trust from Him. Then, and not till then, am I prepared fully to trust your judgment upon live issues. Until then the cleverer you are the more I suspect that your reason will but serve your passions.

It is right that we should pray "God who didst teach the hearts of Thy faithful people by the sending to them the Light of Thy Holy Spirit, grant us by the same Spirit to have a right judgment in all things." The power of right judgment is not a natural heritage but a supernatural achievement. It is from above and not below. If we are to be truly rational on live issues, "we must be born again." It is that true rationality our modern world demands if it is to be saved from destruction. We are full of cleverness, wisdom which comes not from above but is earthly, animal, even devilish, leading to envy, rivalry and all kinds of crooked dealing. But we must have the wisdom—the rationality—which is from above—and which is first of all pure, then peace loving, respectful of personality in others, open to conviction on evidence, with plenty of human kindness in it, based upon an honest life, free from prejudice and insincerity (S. James iii, 15). We must have that. Civilization demands it as a necessity, and we cannot get it, without real religion, an increasing devotion to the one true God and Jesus Christ, whom He has sent—the WORD Who alone brings life to perfect light in men.

CHAPTER V

The Word became Flesh.—S. JOHN i. 14.

SOME Greeks came and asked to see Jesus. The story is never finished. Read it and see (S. John xii. v. 20-32.) We do not know whether they ever saw Him or not. They were brought to Him, but that does not mean that they saw Him. Thousands came to Him and never saw Him at all. He Himself, when He was told that they wanted to see Him, was seized with a sudden agony of soul. He saw Himself as a seed thrown into the ground to rot and to die. His soul was full of trouble. He cried out as it were, "I tell you it is no good, if they want to see Me, they must die. It is no use their coming just to look, they won't see anything but a man, a teacher, another philosopher, and the world is full of them, full of learned talk that flows like a river to be lost in an open empty sea. They must die first. He who holds his life dear is not living at all, only putting off death. It is only those who are content to throw their lives away who can see Me and find eternal life, which is to know the one true God and Jesus Christ whom He has sent. He who sees Me stands face to face with the ultimate reality of all things, all illusions, idols, drugs are taken from him, all his old life must rot within him, rot until it sickens him to look at it, his last vestige of pride must go—he must die, he must give up the idea that he is anything, has anything, can do anything apart from Me. These Greeks, these intellectuals, can never save the world. Their reason only serves their self-assertion. They never see Me, they only see themselves in Me, and that is no good."

No one can save the world who is afraid to die. No one can see Jesus who is afraid to die. That is the terrible truth of His divinity. It was always the same with Him. He cried to men 'Come unto Me,' but when they came He warned them. A rich young man came, 'a thoroughly good fellow' as we say, who had kept the commandments all his life. Jesus loved him, but He did not spare him. "You are all bound up with this money of yours and your position, it is the animal life of the impulses really, self-assertion and self-display, you are still only a semi-intelligent peacock with a big tail. 'Come out of it,' 'Come out of it,' get quit of all this nonsense—and live. Sell all that thou hast and follow me."

A man ran after Him and said he wanted to go to the ends of the earth with Him, and He turned on him with, "The foxes have holes, and the birds of the air have nests—but the Son of Man hath not where to lay His head. It is not what you think it is, following Me. It is like death, loneliness, homelessness. You have got to be alone, I say, you cannot even bring your father and your mother with you, you must learn to hate them if they stand between you and me." You must die first. It is always the same terrible story. Nicodemus going out a bewildered, grey-haired, groping figure, through the darkened streets of the holy city after his talk beneath the stars, muttering to himself, "I must be born again, and I am old—old! How can a man be born again when he is old?"

There is Zacchaeus standing in his office with his books and money bags about—stripping himself naked of everything. "Half my goods I'll give to the poor, and if I have defrauded anyone I will pay him back fourfold." "Dirt," he says, "dirt, you can have the lot, I want Life."

That is what it always meant to see Jesus. No one ever saw Him and remained the man he was before. To those who truly saw Him, He always became, and has always become, the whole meaning of life—the Incarnate WORD.

Who that one moment has the least descried Him,
  Dimly and faintly, hidden and afar,
Doth not despise all excellence beside Him,
  Pleasures and powers that are not and that are.

Ay, amid all men bear himself thereafter,
 Smit with a solemn and a sweet surprise,
Dumb to their scorn and turning on their laughter,
 Only the dominance of earnest eyes?

describes the experience of Zacchaeus, of Nicodemus, and of all who really saw Him in the days of His Flesh, just as truly as it describes the experience of those who saw Him after His Resurrection, and of those countless thousands who have seen Him since by the power of the Spirit. He is the same yesterday—to-day—and for ever—the Incarnate Revelation of the true meaning, value and purpose of all life. There was always Birth—Death—Resurrection—and Ascension in the face of Christ for those who saw Him as He was.

The great Acts of His earthly life were but the expression in time of His eternal nature. He always brought to those who saw Him, a New Birth, an agony of Crucifixion, a Resurrection, and an Ascension, and through that four-fold act of the inmost soul, a conviction of touch with ultimate reality, a new vision of the meaning of the world and of God's creation. Thousands there were who saw Him only with the sensual sight, as the chimpanzee sees the poems of Browning, they tried to use Him to give them food, to satisfy their lust of power and their greed, they touched Him, mauled Him, clawing at Him for themselves, then, when they found He was no use, they tore Him into bleeding pieces and threw Him away. Thousands saw Him with intellectual perception, they asked Him questions, argued with and about Him, tried to get Him on to their side, and use Him for their schemes, and when they found He was no use they led the animals to tear Him limb from limb. But there were those who saw Him with spiritual vision, they saw the spiritual world of Beauty, Truth and Goodness, the world of absolute values, of which He was the WORD—the perfect expression. And for them there was always a New Birth, a Death and Crucifixion; a Resurrection and an Ascension. For those four acts are one in Christ eternally. It is not for nothing that our great Creeds have seized upon the four, and made them the essence of the Gospel.

A speaker at the C.O.P.E.C. Conference at Birmingham complained that those who drew up the Creeds were not interested in the 'Jesus of History.' They paid no attention to His earthly life, they only concerned themselves with His miraculous Birth, His Atoning death, His supernatural Resurrection and Ascension. But we modern men and women had recovered the picture of the historical Jesus, and were mainly concerned with that. In books like "The Jesus of History," by Dr. Glover, we could see once more the gracious human figure as it moved among the Sons of men, converting the sinful, healing the sick, blessing the children. This, he said, and rightly said, was the treasure that modern Scholarship had bestowed upon the Church of God, a portrait of Jesus, drawn and coloured to the life.

No one ought to belittle or despise that portrait. It is the most perfectly beautiful thing in the world. But as we stand before it, and study it, it challenges us, we cannot be content to see it with intellectual perception and appreciation alone, it drives us deeper, and forces us to ask, "What does it mean?" When we lay down these books, even the best of them, we remain unsatisfied. Here is a great fact of History. The great Historical fact. What is its significance? What is its relation to reality? What does it tell us about the meaning of the tragic world in which we live? The books that have been written by the opposite school of thinkers, led by Loisy and Tyrrell, which minimise the importance of the historical figure, saying, indeed, that it is not necessary to think of the picture as being historical at all, since all that matters is the Spiritual Truth it reveals, contain the other side of Truth. To ask whether the portrait is historic or symbolic is to put a false dilemma. If it is historic it must be in the truest sense, symbolic. All history is symbolic, unless the world in which we live is mad and without meaning. If it is true that "right at the heart of the ultimate reality there eternally exists a Person expressing a rational purpose," then that purpose runs through history, and is, in some measure, revealed by every historical event, though much more fully revealed by some events than by others. On the other hand a symbolic picture which is not historic in some sense cannot be known for certain as the symbol of reality.

The portrait is at once historic and symbolic. And it is when we strive to penetrate the symbolic Fact of Christ and discover the Truth symbolized, that we understand why the earlyChristian preachers tore out of the life those four great pictures, and held them up before the world as the essential facts of faith. There is the Babe of Bethlehem, born by the Will of God, there is the broken figure bleeding on the Cross, there is the empty tomb and the Christ that cries across the world, "Behold I am alive for evermore," and there is the calm majestic Lord with wounded hands outstretched to bless ascending into Glory. And these four are One in Christ, and He is the meaning of History, and the revelation of the purpose of the world. It was the WORD that became Flesh, expressing His nature in the terms of our Humanity, it was the WORD—the Person expressing a reasonable purpose through Whom all things came into being, and apart from Whom not a single thing came into being which is of the nature of reality. The history of the world, of mankind, and of each individual soul, is the Birth, The Crucifixion, The Resurrection and Ascension to perfection of that life which is light in men, but light shining in darkness until we all in heart and mind with Him ascend and in Him continually dwell, Who was born on Christmas Day and Ascended into Heaven, the WORD that became flesh.

The first meaning of life, the life both of individuals and of societies, which are but two aspects of one thing, is that it is a New Birth, the coming to birth of that new life, the quality of which in all its beauty was revealed in Jesus Christ; the life which S. John calls eternal life, or the life of the ages. This life, which is mere sensation in the lower creation, becomes coherent thought or consciousness in man, and that consciousness becomes perfect and complete only as it finds its true harmony and unity in Christ, the God in whom reason and religion, experience and the emotion of experience, find their true goal and fulfilment; in Whom and to Whom, therefore, we must all be born again. " For we know that the whole creation groaneth and travaileth in pain together until now, and not only they but ourselves also who have the first fruits of the spirit, we ourselves groan within ourselves waiting for the adoption to wit the redemption of our body."

God coming, God seeking, God being born, God Loving and Giving, giving in all things, and finally in His Son, that is the basis of Christian Truth.

Herein is Love, not that we Loved Him but that He loved us. Advent, the coming of God, is a more accurate and significant name for the creative process than Evolution. To say that the world was made by evolution, if it means anything, merely means that it grew up in an orderly way, but to say that the world was made by Advent or by Christmas, is to say that the meaning, the purpose, and the true value of that orderly growth are revealed in Christ.

So, as our minds swing back bewildered down the vistas of biological and geological time, and we read again the mysterious story of man's past, reaching back to find a kinship with the very stocks and stones, and ask ourselves—what does it mean? Christianity answers, "it means Christmas, the coming of God in Christ." There have been many odd names invented for this " Coming God "—George Bernard Shaw calls Him " the evolutionary urge," the Dean of S. Paul's " some immanent teleology," Bergson " élan vital." All of these cumbrous and pedantic names mean that life looks like, and is the result of, something or someone coming, being born in time, seeking expression in creation. That impression of someone coming grows deeper and deeper as we study the life of men and things, and all these modern inventions bear witness to it; but our faith goes further, as a living faith must do, and declares that the Coming One was, and is, Christ, in Whom all things consist, or hang together, finding a rational significance. The whole of the New Testament is bathed in the light of that Truth. Life has no meaning, apart from the New Birth, the New Life, the life that issues from and gives meaning to the ages—which is in Christ.

Our life so far as it is real is not a sleep and a forgetting, but a coming to birth, a birth which is the act of God.

> Because in tender majesty,
> Thou cam'st to earth nor stayed till we
> Poor sinners stumbled up to Thee,
> I thank my God.
>
> Because the Saviour of us all
> Lay with the cattle in their stall,
> Because the Great comes to the small,
> I thank my God.
>
> Because upon a Mother's breast,
> The Lord of Life was laid to rest,
> And was of Babes the loveliest,
> I thank my God.
>
> Because the Eternal Infinite,
> Was once that naked little mite,
> Because, O Love, of Christmas night,
> I thank my God.

But this New Life means Death to the old. There is, and there always was, as we have seen, death in the eyes of Christ. He is the God of unbearable Beauty that breaks the hearts of men. Bethlehem without Calvary would be no true picture of Life. It could not face its deepest mystery. It is because right at the heart of the Faith there stands this barbarous brutality, that I can cling to it as true to Life as I know it. Life as a New Birth, even though through travail, would not reflect the facts. There is not merely pain, there is cruelty, injustice, torture, exquisite and unmerited agony in every phase of human life. There is not merely sorrow, there is sorrow's crown of sorrow, human sin.

Life demands a Cross as its meaning. When one ponders over the facts, and reads the rolls, of human history and asks, "What does it mean?" "What is God like in Whom it finds its meaning?" Almost, one expects, that broken tortured figure and the bloody sweat upon the ground.

Life is a tragedy. It is impossible to escape from that except by wilful blindness. There is no justice in it, if by justice you mean that pleasure and pain are measured out according to deserving or merit. It is ever the best and bravest who suffer most. Christ was open and honest about that. He never promised men cushions, always a cross. We find that the hardest fact to face up to. We are convinced that we deserve to be justly treated in this life, and that there is something we have a right to be angry about if we suffer injustice. We say we cannot believe in God because of the injustice of the world. Well, if the Christian Faith taught that this world, as we see it, is a just world, and that we get here always what we deserve, I could not believe it. It would be a piteous illusion and a lie. There is no justice in the world as seen by sensual sight or mere intellectual perception. It is useless looking for it. No mere philosophy can justify the ways of God to men. As apprehended by the intellect it is as irrational, as blind, and as brutal as Calvary.

" It is not fair! It is not fair!" Poor souls come and cry out to me, and I hear a voice out of the darkness crying, "My God! My God! Why?" I hear it again and again. A man sentenced to years of imprisonment as the result of an inherited mental disease cries out in rebellion, the good mother of an abandoned son, the innocent girl betrayed and tossed aside, the woman whose hope of Love was murdered on the battlefields of France crying from the unconscious for the child she cannot have, a monotonous interminable procession, some in anger, some sullen, some scornful, some brokenly submissive, but all in the dark and asking Why? The question no mortal man can answer. Yes, it needs a Cross to meet it, and it needs a Christ to bear it and not break. If Christianity tried to explain away all the torture of human life, and to prove that it was just and fair, it would be a heartless mockery, and I would rather go to hell for honest unbelief, than gain the highest heaven by the treachery of faith. But it does not do that. It takes the Cross and plants it in the centre of the world. It says, "I know, there in that wounded writhing Body is the history of the world, the story of man's life on earth. It is as tragic and as terrible as that, but look up, look beyond the Cross to the Christ—and there is the meaning, and the purpose of it all."

He does not ask for pity. He needs none. It is those around the Cross that are piteous, not He who hangs upon it. He knows that. "Father forgive them, they know not what they do." They are in the dark. That is what darkness means. That is the life of mere sensation, of crude instinct and impulse, as it works in men, it is always as obscene and hideous as the crowd about the Cross, sweating, spitting, jeering, lusting with cruel lust of pain, hating and slobbering out their hatred in foul speech, it is always like that, you can see the like in any mob, *or see it in yourself next time you sin*, but look up, "The Light shines in the darkness, and the darkness cannot overcome it." That is what the darkness means to the light, what violence means to reason, what lust means to love, what pride means to humility, suffering like that, but the light can bear the darkness and break through. The New Life can rise above it, triumph over it, trample it under foot, *and that New Life is yours in Him*. He brought it down to earth for you—Who for us men and for our Salvation came down from Heaven, and was Incarnate—the WORD who revealed the quality of eternity in time. That Life is yours in Him, and He is seeking you now that He may give it you. He is seeking you now as I write and you read. I could not write this, if He had not done that. The Cross is God's Word.

As these feeble words are my language ; as through this act in time of pen and ink I seek to reach you, as all I have or am, God help me, is behind this written and rewritten page, so through this act of suffering in time, as language, God seeks you. All that He has, and is, is behind it. It is not that He sought you once in the past, but that He seeks you now in the present. As, when you read these words, they will be a past act of mine, a record of what I was and did on this autumn morning with God's glory of death still golden on the trees, yet I, the living I, will be in them, and they will only help you just so far as the living God is in me, and so far as He takes them and interprets them to you, so, as you stand before the Cross, it is a past act of Jesus Christ in time, a record of what He was and did upon a hill where you may stand outside an earthly city wall, yet He, the living Christ is in it, and it helps you because He was the Very Son of God, and because the urgent Love of God takes it and interprets it to you. Just as these words will be Greek, Hebrew, nonsense to you, unless God uses them now in answer to your prayer, for what I have to say cannot be said, so the Cross will be foolishness, repulsive foolishness to you, unless God speaks through it now. Salvation is always the act of God, but an act through a Word, the WORD of the Cross. *This is the crucial passage in the story of the world, it is the key to the whole book.* The chapters have no sense in them until you come to this. It is written and many waters cannot wash it out. Pilate spoke more truly than he knew, "What I have written I have written," and it has lasted down the ages, "He was crucified under Pontius Pilate." If through these words God finds your soul, it will be because through that Word He first found mine, and showed to me the meaning of Life. So far as they are my words they will fail, so far as they are His Word they will win their way.

On June 7th, 1917, I was running to our lines half mad with fright, though running in the right direction, thank God, through what had been once a wooded copse. It was being heavily shelled. As I ran I stumbled and fell over something. I stopped to see what it was. It was an undersized, underfed German boy, with a wound in his stomach and a hole in his head. I remember muttering, "You poor little devil, what had you got to do with it? not much great blonde Prussian about you." Then there came light. It may have been pure imagination, but that does not mean that it was not also reality, for what is called imagination is often the road to reality. It seemed to me that the boy disappeared and in his place there lay the Christ upon His Cross, and cried, "Inasmuch as ye have done it unto the least of these my little ones ye have done it unto me." From that moment on I never saw a battlefield as anything but a Crucifix. From that moment on I have never seen the world as anything but a Crucifix. I see the Cross set up in every slum, in every filthy over-crowded quarter, in every vulgar flaring street that speaks of luxury and waste of life. I see Him staring up at me from the pages of the newspaper that tells of a tortured, lost, bewildered world.

"Ever and always I can see set up above this world of ours, a huge and towering cross with great arms stretched out East and West, from the rising to the setting sun, and on that Cross my God still hangs and calls on all brave men and women to come out, and share His sorrow and help to save the World."

Red with His Blood the better day is dawning,
Pierced by His pain the storm clouds roll apart,
Rings o'er the earth the Message of the morning,
Still on the Cross the Saviour bears His Heart.

Passionate and low the Voice of God is pleading,
Pleading with men to arm them for the fight,
See how those Hands majestically bleeding
Call us to rout the armies of the night.

But the Vision of Life in the Cross is not a vision of despair, but of confidence and hope, because behind it there is the empty tomb, and the figure with wounded hands outstretched to bless, ascending into glory. That completes The WORD made Flesh which reveals the meaning of Life. Without that we would go mad. We need not, must not feel that death is the end. That is what we are all terrified of—Death. If we are to be born again we must die, we must be crucified with Him, and we feel that, if we do that, if we give up the old life, the lust that burns and stings, the pride that satisfies, the comfort that lulls us into sleep, if we cease to believe in the pleasures of the senses, and the satisfaction of the animal instincts as the true joy of life, there is nothing left, absolutely nothing, that we shall die, and we cannot bear it. A man must have something to live for. Some day, of course, we must give it all up—but not yet. Some day the flesh will grow weary, and the pride of life will wither away, we will grow old, but not yet, time enough when we must; and so we spend our lives postponing death—and clutching greedily all we can get; torturing one another to gobble up all we can snatch from the Table of the Lord. We kick the weaker brother out of the way, or keep him in a foul and filthy cellar out of sight, while we tear with our teeth at the flesh of life. We cook the flesh and lay it daintily before us, we are refined, until the feast is threatened, then we can be as brutal as wolves, prepared to rip and rend that we may live, because we dare not die. The Society papers and all the commercialized system of animal appeal for every class, tell us that the flesh is good. "Eat, you fools—Eat," they say "Women are still soft and white, wine is still red—eat and drink—for there is nothing else—but death." Apart from the satisfaction of the sensual or sensuous desires, we feel that life would be an utter blank, and that is the most terrifying thing in the world. We cannot stand it. We even use the Christian religion sentimentalized as a sop—and imagine we can have everlasting life without death at all. There is no need to die. God is very good-natured and will let us off, has, in fact, let us off because Christ died. We have perverted and distorted the Truth of the Gospel by imagining it to mean that, if we accept death when it is forced upon us, we shall be transported *by the mere act of physical death* into an eternal life which is an extension of this. Whereas Christ was always insisting that the only way to life was *to die here and now for His sake* and the Gospel's, that we may live in Him. We must face that blankness, that nothingness, that feeling that we are giving up everything worth having, and that there is nothing left, in order that we may find Him, and the longer we put it off, the harder it is to do. We must die to live, and we can never do it except through the Power of His Resurrection. It is the Risen and Ascended Christ that saves. The fourfold picture is one in Truth. A new Birth without a Crucifixion is impossible, a Crucifixion without a Resurrection would drive any human being stark staring mad. He would commit suicide, which is the maddest of all mad things, an attempt to murder God. To see the world as a Crucifix without an empty tomb would be a vision too terrible for any human being to look upon, it would drive him, like Judas, shrieking with horror into the night to which there are no stars. We must have the whole faith. The meaning of Life is Advent, Christmas, Good Friday, Easter Day, Ascension-tide, and Pentecost—for the Word became Flesh and dwelt amongst us—and that was the manner of His dwelling.

That is why it is said, "When He went up on High, He led His captives into captivity and gave gifts to mankind." Now this "going up" must imply that He had already "gone down" into the world beneath. He who "came down" is the same as He who "went up"—up beyond the highest heaven that He might fill all things with His Presence—and He it is who gives to the Church true workers of every kind, for the building up of the Body of Christ. And this shall continue until we all attain to that unity which is given by faith, and a fuller knowledge of the Son of God; until we reach the ideal man, the full standard of the perfection of the Christ. Then we shall no longer be like silly children tossed to and fro and blown about by every breath of human teaching, through the trickery and cunning craft of animal men spreading their own deception; but holding the Truth in a Spirit of Love, we shall evolve into complete union with Him Who is our Head, Christ Himself. (Ephes. iv, 8-15). Born—Crucified—Risen and Ascended.

CHAPTER VI

And we beheld His glory.—S. John i. v. 14

We beheld His glory. Here is the individual expression of a corporate experience, the personal testimony to the reality of a new Social life. That is the hall-mark of Christianity. It was in the beginning, is now, and ever shall be, a true community life. The New Birth, the Crucifixion, the Resurrection and Ascension become realities to the soul in and through the Brethren. Always Christ calls men into a company in which they are to find a life different from the life of the world. The Christian witness to the world is to be a new quality of social life, and, so far as there has been any real Christian witness, it always has been that and nothing else. Christian Holiness has never been anything but Love, creating a company of men and women which acted as the Body of Christ filled with His Life, sharing His sufferings, partaking of His triumph, growing with His growth; a body bearing the marks of the Lord Jesus, born, crucified, risen and ascending with Him. A solitary Christian is a contradiction in terms. There never has been such a thing. Men dispute as to whether He founded a Church. And they may well dispute it, if by "founding" a Church they mean mere organizing as we understand it, calling a committee, appointing officers, drawing up rules, issuing propaganda, etc., all the rest of the interminable process by which human societies live and die, a process which may be a process of life or death, according to what it expresses. Its various stages, in some form or other, are inevitable manifestations of human life, and those who despise and ignore them either do not manifest life, or else they reproduce the process and call it by a different name. Protestantism despised the Church and immediately founded innumerable Churches. Human life, wherever it appears, takes a community form, only the life must produce the form, the form cannot produce the life. Eternal life, which is human life made perfect in Christ, does not, and cannot, exist without a community form, but we are mad if we suppose that we can produce the life by making a new form, or maintain it by preserving an old one. We are always trying to do that and failing. Christ did form a committee, appoint officers, draw up rules and issue propaganda. He could not help Himself, and did not want to. He was human. The WORD became Flesh. We are always drawing up new rules because we did not keep the old ones, making a new order because we did not observe the old. We despise the Churches because our souls are sick for the Church. We make new forms because we long for the new Life.

Some suppose that it is the form that kills the life, and so want to do without one altogether. They are filled with contempt and loathing of the poverty-stricken Church they see, and sick with desire for the true one, so they want to destroy all form, and live in the Spirit. God pity the poor dears, lots of us would like to jump out of our skins, but it would not really help us, we could only jump into another one. Even hereafter we are not to be formless Spirits, " there is a natural body, and there is a spiritual body." Often I fear their longing for a formless Church means a deficiency rather than an excess of life, it means, not that they are too good for the Church, but that they are not good enough. They want freedom, but it is often freedom for their pride, their contempt of their neighbours, their resentment of all interference with what they like best. They want to find a Church which will be to them a refuge from their fellow men, especially from the ones they do not like, and there are so many they do not like, that they feel it would be safer not to be bound to any of them, but to worship God alone; with at any rate a minimum of interference from the rest of humanity. It is dreadful to have little curates in black clothes running round trying to be like Jesus Christ, and Bishops in gaiters begging for money to run the Diocese. They do not like meetings and services, they feel nearest to God in the open air, or in an old Church, it must be old, where they can be alone. The truth is that their souls are too refined, and their intelligence too highly cultivated, to stand the vulgarity and triviality of the Church. Of course they do not despise anyone, but they do want to be left alone. This organized religion is revolting, it is death to the spiritual life.

But if your spiritual life is as refined as all that, it is too delicate to live. It is too spiritual to be human. If you are so select that you cannot do with men, you will be missing God Almighty, Who is not nearly so exclusive. The fact of the matter is that you are a fraud, a conscious or unconscious fraud, and what you really want is a Church big enough to contain your own conceit, and there is not one. If you had your way you would find not salvation but the most complete damnation of your soul. You sigh and say:

I would buy me a perfect Island Home,
  Sweet set in a southern sea,
And there I would build me a paradise
  For the heart of my Love and me.

I would plant me a perfect garden there,
  The one that my dream soul knows.
And the years would flow as the petals grow
  That flame to a perfect rose.

I would build me a perfect temple there,
  A shrine where my Christ might dwell.

* * * * * *

And then you would wake to behold your soul
  Damned deep in a perfect Hell.

You could not help it, it would be inevitable. You can only learn to love God as you learn to love your fellowmen. S. John is very blunt about it in his Epistle, and says that if you profess to love God and do not love the Brethren, and he means by that primarily your fellow Christians, you are a liar. "We know that we have passed from death unto life because we love the brethren." The acid test of religious reality is power to produce community life. You cannot have unorganized Christianity, there never has been such a thing, and never will be.

It was upon a company that the Spirit descended at Pentecost, and the first result of that descent was to drive the company out to form a community, which was so filled with the New Life, that they attempted the impossible, and tried to hold all things in common, abolishing private property. And although that sublime and premature effort failed, yet wherever the new life went, there sprang up communities having within them a new power of social unity.

New committees, new rules of life, new red hot propaganda sprang up everywhere. There were conferences at Jerusalem, laws for the Gentile Churches, fiery tracts from S. Peter and S. Paul. There were dissensions and divisions, a wretched sense that the divisions were all wrong, and tremendous efforts to attain to unity. There were all the marks of this dreadful organized Christianity that we have to-day within twenty years of the Crucifixion. There were Priests that went wrong, Judas was the first, and saints that turned out sinners, as in Corinth. But there never was any doubt that Christian Life was a community life, and that the Will of God was the Unity of mankind in Him. Moreover, the idea that somehow or other Christian men and women should hold their goods in common has never ceased to haunt the minds of those who found new Life in Him. They have never been really satisfied with the idea of absolute property. It has always been foreign to their whole conception of life. If Christian Communism was beyond them, at any rate everyone was to look upon what he possessed as a trust from God to be used for the welfare of the Brethren.

Every fresh Revival of the New Life was accompanied by some protest against the system that left untouched extremes of wealth and poverty. Monasticism was an attempt to realize the perfect Christian Community, a life in which men could work and earn their bread to the glory of God, and for the love of the Brethren.

The score of heretical sects that arose in the middle ages, such as the Waldenses, the Albigenses, the Beghards, the Brethren of the Common Lot, were all efforts to maintain a new order of Social life, in which men might live as Brethren, working for the common good. They failed, but then the whole of Christianity is one long record of failure, it will never succeed until we all are one in Him. All Life is a failure, a reaching beyond what we can grasp, an attempt to achieve the apparently impossible—a Birth, a Crucifixion, but a Resurrection, and an Ascension.

They may have failed but apparently whenever Christ touches men they are stirred to try again. *This dream of a new and better social order is as much an essential part of the Christian Life as prayer, and communion with God.* Like them it has had its ups and downs. It has been crucified with the life of prayer, all down the ages, but it has risen again to challenge the world, and set men striving after better things. Men cannot meet with Christ in prayer, and remain content to shut Him out of the places where they earn their bread, and live their common life. The Christian life of devotion and the Christian ideal of community life are inextricably bound up with one another, and stand or fall together.

Right at the heart of the Christian Devotional Life there has always been the Breaking of Bread, and when that Sacrament is divorced from the dream of a Christian Social order, it is deprived of its true significance. If we cut off that Bread which is His Body from all connection with our daily bread, and the means whereby we earn it; if we declare that He is present in the Bread of the Sanctuary, but absent from the bread of the street—we deny the Truth of the Incarnation. We deny that "The WORD became Flesh—through Whom, all things were made, and without Whom nothing was made that was made." The Christian Faith demands that we acknowledge a real presence of Christ in the Bread upon the Altar before it is broken and consecrated. We cannot deny that presence without denying that Christ is the Word of God through Whom the worlds were made, and in Whom they find their meaning.

It is this presence of Christ in common bread and His concern with the way we earn it that the world denies emphatically. They are quite willing, the men of the world, to allow that we may find Him, by an act of faith, in that Bread upon the altar, so long as we do not drag Him in to the bread of the common street. Nobody worries about Christ so long as He can be kept shut up in Churches, He is quite safe there, but there is always trouble if you try to let Him out.

The late Bishop of Zanzibar told a great body of Christians that they must " fight for their tabernacles." If that means, as on his lips it did, that we must stand firm for the Truth that the tabernacle of God is with men; if it means that the gates of the little shrine, where men and women come to worship the Christ, are set open wide that He may go out to seek and to save, it is well; but if it means that we confine Him, and seek Him only there among the lilies, it is a dangerous deceit indeed. To confine Christ is to crucify Him. Christ can be crucified in Churches, and the clouds of incense may but serve to hide the sorrow in His eyes.

The first necessity of the Christian Faith is to accept Christ as the meaning of all things, and to see all things only as they are seen in Him. In Him is life, all life, even the life of common bread. Through Him were all those powers given by which men earn and eat to-day. Through Him were made the monster ships by which the grain is brought to us, through raging storms across three thousand miles of sea. The loaf we break, the wafer that we consecrate, was born, may be, in the golden miles of Canada, America, or the Argentine, and is gathered for us from the ends of the earth, for all the world is one in bread. If it were not for that new world-wide unity in bread, millions who live to-day would have to die, they could not keep themselves. It is a due development of man. It was the sowing and reaping of a harvest that first turned the nomad hunter, who ranged the forest for his food, like a lion slaying for his cubs, into the settled social tiller of the soil. There never was a harvest until men learned in some measure to work as one. Bread has always been an artificial thing, and is now as artificial as Quaker oats. The throb of the screws, the flames of the blast furnace, the gloom and darkness of the mine, are all in our daily bread. As it lies there upon the altar it is the oblation of our whole intricate and manysided life, the sweat, and the blood, and the brain of man are in it, men for whom Christ died. The lives of toiling millions go to make the pure white wafer or the little piece of Bread we hold up before the Lord before the Consecration act, and therefore Christ is in it, or more accurately it is in Christ, and has no meaning apart from Him. *The whole of our Social Order is in the Bread of the Altar which waits the act of the Christian community who lift it up to God.*

We cannot emphasize too strongly the fact that it is the Christian Community that consecrates, it is a corporate act, in which every member of the Church takes part. It is not consecrated by the priest for the people of God, but by the people, the Church which is His Body, through the Priest the Church ordains. It is a corporate act, and that is its very essence. Here then is the Christian community seeking by God's grace to consecrate the Social Order of common life, that it may become the Sacrament of His Presence among men.

What then is the Relation between the presence of Christ in common bread, which the doctrine of the Incarnation compels us to acknowledge, and that Presence which our Christian experience compels us to call, with reverence and gratitude, The Real Presence of the Lord in the Sacrament?

The Presence of Christ in the Bread, and in the present Social Order which is the meaning of the Bread, is *the presence of the Crucified*. Can we doubt that?

There never was a time when there was not sin and sorrow in Bread,* and there is sin and sorrow in it now—such sin and such sorrow, the sin of slums and the sorrow of the darkened lives that cry for light from the underworld. All sorrow is His sorrow, and, mystery of mysteries, all sin is His sin, who was made sin for us. When, therefore, the Christian community, through its own appointed Priest, holds up the Bread, they hold up the Crucified Lord. They shew forth His death till He come. They identify themselves with Him in His age long agony of Redemption, and confess with sorrow their part in the sin that mars the winning of our Daily Bread. The lust of power, the faithless fear, the hatred, and the bestial greed which break the world wide unity of Bread, and make what God wills to be a beautiful and balanced order into a cruel, ugly chaos.

No man can eat alone. The very act of eating brings us into touch with our brothers and with Him. He seeks, it is His eternal nature to seek us in the breaking of all Bread. But the shame of our common life is that we eat and drink not discerning the Lord's Body. We snatch at His gifts like lower animals, seeing only with sensual sight, seeing in the Bread we eat neither the Brethren nor the Christ, but ourselves, and our own lust of life. Thus it is that we eat and drink damnation to our souls, and the Bread of Blessing is turned into a curse. There is the snarl as of dogs in our cities, and the cry of the child in our streets. He seeks us in the common bread, but cannot find us. He could not cease to seek us. If for one millionth part of a second His everlasting search should cease, the stars would fall upon us, and the hills would crumble into dust. For the Life of the Universe is the Love of God. It needs no Church nor Sacrament to secure God's Love for us, or to make it certain that the Eternal Shepherd will come seeking His sheep. That is His Nature, and He could not be false to Himself.

* cf. S. James Epistle, Chap. v. 4.—Behold the hire of the labourers who have reaped down your fields, which is of you kept back by fraud, crieth: and the cries of them which have reaped are entered into the ears of the Lord of Sabaoth.

That is the central Truth of the New Testament Revelation. God is not the Eastern Monarch on His Throne waiting for the world to come to Him, He is an ever active Spirit of Eternally living Love, seeking to Create and to Redeem. God seeks, but before we can be found of Him, there must be from us response. However faint and poor it be, yet there must be some answer to His call. While we are yet a great way off—He runs—but we must first have said, "I will arise and go." The sin that turns the blessing of our Daily Bread, and the means whereby we earn it, into a curse, is that we earn and eat it without a thought of Him. As we have seen, He is seeking us through this New Environment which He has created, the world wide economic unity, which He has made to be the body of the Brotherhood of man, but we do not answer, we see nothing in it but increased power to gratify our lusts, and so the Body is broken, wounded, torn, it bleeds on battlefields, is diseased in slums, it is covered with festering sores of vulgar luxury, it groans with hunger, and is rent by strife.

This is His Body, in more than a symbolic sense, and it is in the common bread of the oblation before the consecration act. We make too little of the offertory, it is not understood. Money has degraded it, and it has become the collection to pay the verger to stoke the furnace and keep our feet warm while we pray. But in truth we ought to offer up our money too, remembering that money is human flesh and blood, a measure of human energy, physical, mental, and moral in the last analysis. It is not an evil or a sordid thing in itself. There is no greater blessing, nor anything more beautiful than a sound and stable monetary system. The complex network of our modern finance ought to be the healthy nervous system of the Body of Mankind. Contempt of and misuse of money is contempt of and misuse of man, and therefore of God. The sordidness of money is in ourselves, and the kind of shame we have about it is a sign of something wrong deep down within our private and our public life. We always come down to money, we do not lift it up. That is why our very charity has become a curse, a sop to our uneasy consciences, a means whereby we protect ourselves from pain. The offertory has become a joke, and the joke is the sign of the nasty trivial nature of our social life. We snigger about our offering, as I doubt not the Jews that pressed about Him sniggered at the Christ. The perfunctory offering of alms that cost us nothing is a sign of the divorce of the Sacrament from the daily life. It is time we ended that. The alms and the oblations are one—two sides of one thing—which is the Body of the Lord. God is seeking us through money, its power ought to be the power of His Love, and never until it is to us the Sacrament of our unity in Him, can the world find Peace. The misuse of money is the deepest root of War.

In our common life Christ seeks us through Bread and Money, which is another form of Bread, and men do not respond, and therefore He is crucified afresh. *But in the Sacrament we do respond.* The Christian community meets to break the Bread and offer alms in memory and for Love of Him. They are met to plead His Sacrifice, and to identify themselves with His suffering in and for the world. They join in a Confession of our common sin, their part in it, and their sorrow for it. That is the meaning of the General Confession. Men have got it all mixed up with their private confessions, and, having but a feeble sense of their own sinfulness, have thought that the solemn words " the burden of them is intolerable " ought to be cut out, because they could not say them with sincerity. But it is not the fact that you lied or evil lusted last week that is intolerable, though it ought to be, it is the procession of prostitutes, the squalor of Bethnal Green, the anguish of children and the torture of women, it is the sin of the world that is intolerable. If you have not begun to feel that, you have not begun to know Him.

Is it not intolerable ? O, God in heaven, if you do not know it—go and see. If you still think life is as tidy and neat as your Sunday altar, looking so nice with its lilies and cross, go and see—you must know the tragedy of the altar before you find its Peace. The man whose eyes God has opened sees Christ crucified in the world, and enters into the fellowship of His sufferings, becoming a sin-bearer for His sake.

That is what it means to be a member of a Church. 'I fill up in my body what is lacking of the sufferings of Christ for His body's sake, which is the Church' (Col. i, 24). This is at once the joy and sorrow of the Christian life.

> Gladness be with thee helper of the World,
> Methinks this is the authentic sign and seal
> Of Godship that it ever waxes glad,
> And more glad, until gladness blossoms, bursts
> Into a rage to suffer for mankind
> And recommence at sorrow.

Whenever the Church has been alive with His life it has felt this burden of the world's sin, and this is the very Sacrament of sin bearing, in which the Brethren acknowledge their part in the world sin, and identify themselves with the suffering of the world's Saviour. In it they take the common bread in which they perceive the presence of the Crucified and lift it up, lift it up by a corporate act of honest Love, seeking in it not themselves, but Him, not their will but His Will, not their gain but His glory. *And because they lift it up, and every time it is so lifted up, He can and does take it and use it, as He can use no other Bread,* use it to become in fact His Body, the instrument of a Presence which is a real Presence in a unique and special sense, because it is the Presence of the Christ not merely Born and Crucified as He is in all the world, but Risen and Ascended too—*the Presence of the Christ with Power.* That is why this corporate act, whereby the Bread is lifted up, has ever been the sum and centre of the Christian worship, in which they have always found and find the meaning of their lives. In it they pledge themselves, and are endowed with power, to go out and suffer with Him, bearing in Love and striving in prayer against the sin of the world, that men may be led to lift up all bread, and all the means whereby they earn it, seeking in them not themselves but Him, seeking first the Kingdom of God and His Righteousness that all things may be added to them, that so they may eat and drink salvation to their souls and bodies, and, living with eyes unveiled, in a Sacramental universe, may everywhere discern the Body of the Lord.

But where worship is divorced from work, and God's Presence in the Sanctuary from His presence in the street, we run the deadly danger of localizing God, and our Sacraments may be turned into sin. If the Sacrament is to take its proper place as the central act of Christian Worship, Christian men must learn to see in it the whole purpose and meaning of their daily work, and that means that the whole multitude of gifts and powers whereby we earn and eat must be lifted up from the level of use for private profit to the level of use for the Glory of God. Until that is done the Church must continue to suffer and to strive, bearing the sin of the world, she must continue "to show forth the Lord's Death, till He come," come with the Power of the Risen and Ascended Christ to all men, as He comes to the faithful soul who eats His Body and drinks His Blood."

We must not interpret the sacred words "The Body of our Lord Jesus Christ, which was given for thee, preserve Thy Body and Soul unto Everlasting Life" as though Everlasting Life only began beyond the grave, and in the world to come." It begins here and now. It is the true community of life of Love, without which whosoever liveth is counted dead before Him, and which it is our duty to manifest in our bodies and our souls for the saving of mankind.

He that hath the Son hath—not shall have but hath— everlasting life, and that life must progressively permeate and be expressed in every activity of man, until the Kingdoms of this world become the Kingdom of our God and of His Christ. Thus in the Blessed Sacrament is summed and centred the Power, the meaning, and the purpose of our Christian life. Through it we enter into the Fellowship of His sufferings that we may rise and ascend with Him in work that is worship, and worship that is our most glorious work, living our lives in praise and prayer, for:

Peace does not mean the end of all our striving,
  Joy does not mean the drying of our tears,
Peace is the power that comes to souls arriving
  Up to the light where God Himself appears.

Joy is the wine that God is ever pouring,
  Into the hearts of those that strive with Him,
Opening their eyes to vision and adoring,
  Strengthening their arms to warfare glad and grim.

Bread of Thy Body give me for my fighting,
  Give me to drink Thy Sacred Blood for Wine,
While there are wrongs that need me for the righting,
  While there is warfare splendid and divine.

Give me for light the sunshine of Thy sorrow,
  Give me for shelter the shadow of Thy Cross,
Give me to share the glory of to-morrow,
  And gone from my heart is the bitterness of loss.

CHAPTER VII

The Glory of the only Son sent from the Father.—S. JOHN i. 14

GLORY is one of the great words which cannot be defined. It is not possible to say what it means. Not because it means too little but because it means too much. It is one of the words that are used at points where human speech fails, as an attempt to express the inexpressible.

There are many such words in every language, and they have always been great powers in the world. Liberty, Justice, Honour, Equality, Progress, all have this in common that they defy definition. Libraries have been written to define them, but they remain like mountain peaks refusing to be climbed. The Truth is that they all penetrate beneath the reason and the intellect to that underworld of the human mind wherein the primitive passionate forces of life, the impulses and instincts, exercise their vital power for good or ill. It is for this reason that they are great fighting words. Whenever men are called to battle they are used like drums and trumpets to sound the challenge and stir the blood of men to war. They are the words for which men slay and suffer death. That is why the reckless use of them is mortal sin. They are not words which should be used without a solemn sense of responsibility. The man who plays with them is playing with what Dr. William McDougall calls, "the central mystery of life and mind and will."

They are the religious words in the strict sense, that is, words which either drive men mad or raise them to the highest sanity, or, if the soul be dead or sleeping, elicit no response at all, and have no meaning. In periods when the primitive passions of men are roused and they are living fiercely, the great words are wantonly misused, as they have been in the last ten years. They have been scattered broadcast to gratify the passion of the panic-stricken mob, thrown like pearls before swine. The result of this has been what our Lord foresaw, familiarity breeds contempt, and the great words have become suspected and despised. The world to-day is weary of them, and scents insincerity whenever they are used, and not without reason. The speech of the politician and the demagogue is often as bitter as brine to the soul athirst for Truth, nor is that bitterness of empty speech always absent from the pulpit, which may account for the antagonism or indifference of the pew. Great words tempt the speaker, that is why he needs to say his prayers, and glory is one of them. There is a false glory that is not His. We went to war for glory and found no glory in war, and thousands to-day will tell you that there is no glory in life at all. They are disillusioned and disappointed, the fires of life are burning low. But that will not last, it is a phase that must pass and is already passing. Man does not die, and he must either find some glory in life or perish self-destroyed.

You Christians are always singing hymns, a man said to me the other day, I suppose they are all about heaven for I do not see anything on earth to sing hymns about. He was not properly alive, you could see he was not. He was killed in June, 1917, when his son was shattered by a shell near Ypres. There were many casualties that never appeared in the lists. But men cannot live for long without something to sing about, something to praise in poetry, to celebrate in colour, or to bow their knees and worship in the silence of pure joy. They must have glory, for glory is what sets a man singing, dancing, painting, praying, writing poetry, pouring himself out in joyous sacrifice, or makes him bow his head in dumb and wondering awe. The permanent danger of mankind is not no glory, but false glories. The Bible—which is the book of human life, the only completely human book because it goes not only down into hell, but up into heaven, meets man's sin with God's Redemption, contains both Judas and Jesus, the almost less than human with the humanly divine,—the Bible is full of glories.

Everything that has ever made man's heart beat faster, and stirred the blood within his veins is there, all the many sided glory of man's life on the earth. Glory of riches, glory of power, glory of glittering thrones, great temples, towering mountains and tall trees. Glory of sun and moon and stars, the glory of a woman's hair, glory of white lilies and pure saints, glory of gallant horses and great beasts, glory of youth and glory of age, glory of morning, glory of eve, glory of cities, nations, empires, armies, kings, all the thrill and throb of passionate life, the Bible knows it all. But there is no cry that it contains so full of exaltation, trembling reverence, triumphant certainty and joy unbounded as this, "We beheld His glory, glory as of the only Son sent from the Father's side," or the cry of S. Paul, "God who commanded the light to shine out of the darkness hath shined into our hearts to give the light of the knowledge of the glory of God in the Face of Jesus Christ."

And in a thousand different forms, in passionate poetry, majestic music, in a blaze of perfect colour, in mysteries of arch and aisle, in splendour of white steeples, and strength of massive towers, the cry has been echoed down the ages—thine is the glory for ever and ever, Amen. It is in Bach's Mass in B Minor. It is in the spire of Salisbury and the towers of York. Words fail me. What more can I say. Just the steady, sober Truth of my own soul lost in the dark without Him:

Only in Him can I find home to hide me,
  Who on the Cross was slain to rise again.
Only with Him my comrade God beside me
  Can I go forth to war with sin and pain.

The glory of Jesus Christ—what is it? What picture was in S. John's mind as he wrote. Was it the picture that he painted elsewhere, " His head and His hairs were white like wool, as white as snow, and His eyes were as a flame of fire, and when I saw Him I fell at His feet as dead. And He laid His right hand upon me, saying, Fear not; I am the first and the last." Or did His mind swing back to the mount of Transfiguration, to the Jesus Whose face did shine as the sun and Whose raiment was white as the light. If we are to judge by the story which follows, the Gospel according to S. John, it is to neither of these points that his mind turns, but to the hill outside the city, and to the central Cross, and the figure hanging serenely patient in His agony upon it. Even more than the others the fourth Gospel is dominated by, and finds its denouement in, the Passion. It is at the crowning point of the Passion that he breaks out again into a direct personal testimony " He that saw it bare record, and his record is true, and he knoweth that he saith true, that ye might believe." " But one of the soldiers with a spear pierced His side, and forthwith came there out Blood and Water," " and we beheld His glory, glory as of the only begotten of the Father—full of grace and truth." And this is borne out by the fact that in another place, when he is looking into the great distances as far as the eyes of inspired faith can see, when he is trying to express what he sees in the very heart of God, he cries, " And I beheld, and lo in the midst of the throne . . . stood a Lamb as it had been slain . . . and I heard the voice of many angels round about the throne, and the number of them was ten thousand times ten thousand, and thousands of thousands, saying in a loud voice, ' Worthy is the Lamb that was slain to receive power and riches, and wisdom, and strength, and honour, and glory and blessing.' " The glory of all the great words finds its only meaning in the glory of the WORD who became Flesh—the Lamb that was slain from the foundation of the World.

It was the Cross that was the glory centre of the Christ for St. John. It was through the Cross that the gates of the highest heaven were opened wide and he could see within, and in that heaven's very heart he saw the Crucified. That is the central Truth of the Christian Faith, and the hardest Truth to bear. Men have never been able to stand it, they cannot stand it now—the deity of the Lamb. A helpless, harmless, unarmed God who bears no sword, and wields no force to drive men to His Will, has never seemed like God to men. He does not seem like God to-day. We are all in our hearts like Peter, and when God bares His very soul and shows the wounds, and sorrow there—the suffering of Perfect Love—we say, "This be far from Thee, Lord," and we do it for the same reason as S. Peter—we make God in the image of man. "You are thinking not the thoughts of God, but the thoughts of men." We think of the Christ in glory as different from the Christ who came in great humility. We give to Christ in Heaven what He would not have on earth, a monarch's throne, a golden crown, and force to coerce and compel men to His Will. We cannot understand any king but Caesar, so we Caesarise the Christ. We cannot worship what we do not fear, and so we make Christ terrible as tyrants are, and clothe Him in the panoply of our earthly kings. Men have always done this. They made God in their own image, and so saw His glory as the glory of force, of power to dominate and compel. God was the supreme unlimited, untrammelled Egotist with omnipotent force to work His Will. He was what man the egotist would like to be—the absolute man in the street. The glory of absolute force has always thrilled men, and thrills them still. We love the strong, dominant, driving man, he is what we would like to be—and we naturally worship the Napoleon of eternity.* He can do what we would like to do, damn all our enemies to hell, and punish them as they deserve. We cannot slay the men who differ from us, so we imagine One who can and will. We are like the little maid of all work in the kitchen who dreams of Lady Ermyntrude and

* That was the secret of the popular adoration of Lord Kitchener at the beginning of the War. He was pictured as the man of Power who swept obstacles out of his way with a wave of his hand. That strong face with the slight cast in the eyes summed up in itself all that we wanted to be. Therefore his name was a name to conjure with. He was the apotheosis of ourselves. God rest his soul. We laid a heavy burden on his back.

the Duke of Abercrombie, with coronets, and strings of pearls. She leaves her sordid life on earth, and walks a stately duchess in a splendid drawing-roon, ordering her servants with calm and haughty certainty that they must obey. The God we naturally worship is an infinite extension of ourselves—a God Who is what we would be if we could have our way—and so we make Him an absolute Monarch.

We cannot believe that God is like Christ, so we make Christ like God to compensate. We are still mostly Greeks or Jews to whom the Cross is either foolishness or a stumbling block. We are a proud, independent, self-reliant people, and have never been happy with Christ crucified as revealing the glory of God. To us it would degrade God and demean His dignity to suppose that He was harmless, and could not hurt anyone physically. What we think is, " Christ was meek and gentle once, just to give us a chance, but now He is gone up on high, and when He comes again it will be altogether different. He will come in glory, and of course that means with a sword and a host of heavily-armoured angels, and torments for the wicked in His hands." So we interpret the passages that tell us of His coming, in power and great glory, as though His power and His glory could change their nature, and from being the power of Love become the power of force and fear, and from being the glory of service and humility become the glory of domination and pride. Christ was Jesus once on earth but when He comes again He will be like God, a super-super-Napoleon. Thus we do not see the glory of Christ, but give Him a glory of our own.

We do this inevitably until we really see Him. Then we realize that it is not Christ that changes His glory but we that must change ours. It is not He that assumes the glory of force but we that must progressively perceive the glory of Reason and of Love. He is the same yesterday, to-day, for ever, there never has been, and there never can be, any change in Him, but we must change until we cease to fear force, admire despots, and grovel in abject worship before the tyranny of massed armies and organized mobs, and learn to worship the Love, the pure and peaceable wisdom, and the selfless humility of Christ—His glory as of the only Son, sent from the Father's side. We are redeemed as we learn that the folly of God is wiser than men, and the weakness of God is stronger than men. For the Word of the Cross is to those who are perishing—not living but striving to postpone death—pure folly—but to those who are on the road of life it is the Power of God. To those who are still living on the level of sensual sight or of the material intellect the way of Love and Reason is just madness (cp. Chap. iv), but to those who live on the level of spiritual vision, it is the only sanity.

As, through evolution in time, the true nature of the world in which we live is progressively revealed to us, it becomes more and more evident that we can only live in it as we conform to the Christian standard and attain to the Christian Virtues (Chap. ii). History is working itself out to a crisis, and the necessity of a choice between the glory of the Cross and the glory of the world, becomes more and more urgent. Through the vast complexities of our modern civilized world made one by God, the Crucified Christ is looking down upon us—with death in His bleeding hands and feet– but life in the light of His burning eyes—and demanding from us all—every individual man and woman—a choice between the glory of Reason, Patience, and Love, and the glory of Force, and Wrath and Fear.

The European man whom the Dean of S. Paul's describes as "the fiercest of the beasts of prey, who is not likely to abandon the weapons which have made him the lord and bully of the planet," is threatened with extinction and disaster unless he either becomes a more tyrannous lord, and a more bestial bully, using without restraint or remorse the powers of destruction that have been put into his hands, or dies with Christ and finds a more excellent way. There are many modern thinkers who call upon us loudly to take the way of the world, and take it with vigour, to close our ranks against the common foe, which is the coloured races and the submerged masses of the world, to reassert our natural supremacy, brush aside all scruples, and boldly adopt a thorough-going policy of world-wide domination and repression. We still have the power to terrorize, and if necessary, exterminate the weaker brother from the world. " Progress," they say, " depends upon the strong man, and the strong peoples ; in God's name, the old name of Jehovah, Lord of Hosts, not this decadent new name of Jesus, Lord of Mercy, let them use their strength, before the brutal rabble of all lands rise up in their incurable and inevitable animal blindness, and destroy the culture that the exceptional men have laboriously produced by the exploitation of the foolish masses of mankind."

It is evident even to these men that the sands of time are running out, and that we must decide. What shall we do with the man Christ Jesus, put Him to death as a silly-dreaming fool, Who betrays and cannot save the world, or hail Him King of Kings, and Lord of Lords, the only Ruler of peoples. We must do one or the other, unless we are to drift to our destruction. At present we are drifting. We are doing neither the one nor the other. We are putting our trust in force and fear, but not whole-heartedly. The strong man is asserting his rights but his hand trembles, and he is not sure. There are powers that hold him back. Force begets force, and domination breeds rebellion. What he calls the rabble of the world, at home and abroad, is massing itself to organized resistance. The European man lives in a house divided against itself, the weaker brother over here feels himself nearer to the weaker brother over there in the East, than he does to the strong of his own race. There is division at home, and the strength of the West is being dissipated in class and national antagonisms. From the Asiatic point of view there is a two-fold civil war in Europe, its own strong men are warring with the weak. Moreover the strong man is not what he was. That strange man on the Cross worries him, he is uncomfortable about Christ. Just when he is going to strike, a hand is laid on his arm, and even though he shakes it off and strikes, the blow has not his whole force behind it, it wounds but it does not kill. Christ is making cowards of us all. We dare not do wrong thoroughly. We are not as good murderers as we were. We have begun to apologize for our existence, and seek to justify ourselves.

That is fatal. It is really fatal. We cannot save the world by timid murder, and mild force. The prospect that opens out before us when we contemplate the full use of our powers, terrifies us. There are thousands who pray for a strong man who would not dare to follow him if he came. They worship Napoleon but are frightened of Christ. He hangs there on His cosmic Cross, terrible as an army with banners, because He bleeds, bleeds in the slums, and in the unemployed, bleeds in the little children crammed into the mills of India, China and Japan, bleeds in the subject races made into instruments of gain, bleeds in the memory of our "glorious dead," in Jack and Edward who went out to fight for Freedom, Honour and Peace, and are waiting for them still. We are like the Englishman in Bernard Shaw's S. Joan, who was not saved by the sufferings of Christ until he saw them in the Agony of S. Joan, and then was not so much saved as shattered.

Something has come over us all. We are not the men we were. But we will recover, the strong men say. It is only a passing phase. The good old times will come back again. It is only shell shock. This milk and water sentiment will die out, and we shall recover our nerves, take up the white man's burden, and go out to rule and punish. I wonder. I wonder. I am frightened of Christ. I think those who rage and spit on Him, who declare defiantly that He is dead and done for, those who caricature and curse Him, as the terrified rulers of Russia, and the strong men here at home do, scorning the Sermon on the Mount as an impossible dream; I think their fear of Him, which is manifest in their defiance, is nearer the Truth than the indifference of those who think He does not matter. He is really dangerous. If He is not the Son of God, and the revelation of reality, He is a most pernicious impostor. It is really true that "the white man with his genius for leadership and fighting is in danger of extinction." He must either kill Christ or

Christ will kill him with His glory of justice, reason, patience and peace.

He looks as contemptible as ever with His ragged rabble of Church that shouts Hosanna on Sunday and runs from the Garden of Gethsemane on Friday, that protests like Peter and then betrays, that disputes who shall be greatest and thinks it is extravagant to wash men's weary feet; with His crowd of wretched parsons, poor human fools like me, who preach the Gospel and cannot live it, who try to be loving and are not even amiable. He is as ridiculous as ever, just the same Christ that sat with a dirty purple horse cloth on His bleeding back, and a crown of thorns set sideways on His head, with a mock sceptre in His hand, and the spittle of a drunken soldier rolling down His face, just the same Christ, but I am afraid of Him, as, in his heart of hearts, I believe the European Man, the fiercest of the beasts of prey, is frightened of Him. He is disturbing, unnerving, He saps self-confidence and murders pride. He makes men want to go down upon their knees, and no strong man should do that except to the Almighty. That, of course, is all right. All men must kneel before the Almighty—He is the force of all forces, the Tyrant of tyrants, Who can destroy all the worlds in a moment of time. Even the bully may bow to a bigger bully than himself and remain a bully still.

But this Jesus unmans us. Just when we are going to assert our proper rights, and claim our own position, He comes and looks at us, and asks us awkward questions as to whether our rights are right, and whether we have any position. He is dangerous. He takes the fight out of a man. I can hear the fiercest of beasts of prey pleading for mercy. "O Man upon the Cross don't look like that, it hurts, let me live a little longer for myself, life is very pleasant, and even the milder lusts are good. I will be respectable and civilized, I will cover up my murders and decently disguise my robbery and theft; but go away, go away and leave me. I am only a sinful man, and my sins are very sweet. Why do You come and torment me. It is absurd asking me to kill myself like this. What have You got to give in exchange for my honest pride, my proper self-reliance and self-respect. I won't listen or look. You will ruin the world with those eyes, paralyzing the powers of law and order, and threatening commerce and trade. You cannot expect us to think about natives when we want land and raw materials, or to worry ourselves about men when we want to make money." But He will not go away. I do not believe He will let us alone. He is making us waver all over the world. He even got into the Treaty of Versailles. He is going to drive us to a decision with His wounded hands. He will not let us have His world for a playground, a battlefield, a factory, or an Empire any longer, we must give it to Him. *We must give it to Him or—or there will be darkness over all the earth from the sixth hour until the ninth—and that may be a thousand years.* We must decide, and this decision is for you and me. The history of the world is played out in the human soul, the individual human soul. The fate of the world, our children and our children's children, depends on you and me.

That is the meaning of this Lent. As He looks down upon you—with anxious wonder in His eyes—He sees the world in you. He thinks the world of every one of us. Are you going to try and keep the world for a playground—in which you have a good time, a battlefield on which you strive for your own personal ambitions, a factory to make wealth for you to spend, an Empire to satisfy your pride, or are you going to give it up to Him. Half measures are no good. Compromise without repentance and consecration will not save you or the world. It is the surest way to destruction. If all your Christ can do for you is to turn you into a caged beast, a respectable sinner, a half-hearted servant of the old red lusts, you cannot save your soul alive, or save the world in which you live. It is a personal matter—yet not a purely personal matter. You live in a world and a world yet lives in you. For God's sake do not think you do not matter, you are all that matters, for you are in all, and all is in you. Make up your mind—do *you* believe in the glory of Christ—as of the only Son sent from the Father's side?

Is God Love and Reason, or is He brute force and self-assertion ? Is Christianity true or is it a tissue of dangerous sentimentality ? Can it save or will it ruin the world ? It is manifestly dangerous. If it is not true, as a revelation of reality, it is likely to bring a curse upon the world. Christ is either divine or decadent. If He disarms and debrutalizes the western beast of prey, and makes him ashamed of his teeth and claws, and the world is in reality a jungle where brute force alone makes for survival, and self-assertion is the great necessity for life, then this Prince of Peace will be responsible for an orgy of bloodshed the like of which has never been. It is absurd to ignore Him. He ought either to be worshipped or crucified quickly before it is too late. If He cannot redeem mankind, and make them reasonable then He will ruin them body and soul. The question of all questions is this. Do you believe that the way of reason, self-sacrifice, service and love is the way of life for you, and all mankind ? Do you believe that in reality this world is not a battle-field for opposing armies, but a home for a family ? Are you prepared to risk your life and your children's lives, and to stake the honour of your country on that Faith ? Will you risk Good Friday to win an Easter Day ?

Lord, I believe, help thou mine unbelief. I look upon the world and I see a Baby on a Mother's Breast, a Body broken on a Cross, an Empty Tomb with a great stone rolled away, and One like unto the Son of Man with wounded hands outstretched to bless ascending in His Glory ; and I believe that, right at the heart of the ultimate reality there was in the beginning, is now, and ever shall be, world without end, a Person expressing a rational purpose which men can in some measure understand. I believe that this Person was, is, and ever shall be with God, and indeed is God, though it is nearer the Truth to say "with God," for "the Father is greater than He." I believe that through this Person all things came into being, and that, apart from Him, not a single thing came into being which is of the nature of reality. In Him are the eternal sources of life, that life which from the darkness of mere sensation becomes light of intelligence in men, a light shining in darkness which cannot overcome it. I believe that this Person took upon Himself, and expressed Himself through, our human nature, and lived out a human life among men, and that they beheld, and can now behold, His glory which is the glory of the only perfect expression of Love, which is the ultimate and absolute reality of all things.

Lord I believe!
Man is no little thing,
That, like a bird in Spring,
Comes fluttering to the Light of Life,
And out into the darkness of long death.
The Breath
Of God is in him,
And his agelong strife
With evil has a meaning and an end.
Though twilight dim
His vision be,
Yet can he see
Thy Truth.
And in the cool of evening Thou, his friend,
Dost walk
With him, and talk
(Did not the Word take Flesh?)
Of the great destiny,
That waits him, and his race
In days that are to be.
By grace
He can achieve great things,
And, on the wings
Of strong desire,
Mount upward ever, higher and higher,
Until above the clouds of earth he stands,
And stares God in the Face.
Amen and so be it.

BRISTOL: BURLEIGH LTD., AT THE BURLEIGH PRESS